ALISON PRINCE

A Spy at Mill Green

Armada

An Armada Original

A Spy at Mill Green was first published in the U.K.
in 1983 in Armada by Fontana Paperbacks,
8 Grafton Street, London W1X 3LA.

Printed in Great Britain by
William Collins Sons & Co. Ltd., Glasgow

Contents

CHAPTER 1

Creepy Kritz

"The architect who built this place must have been a twit," said Danny. He stared out of the bus window as they approached the gates of Mill Green School on Monday morning. A gang of men were digging up the drive which led to the school building.

"It's stupid," agreed Rachel, nodding her curly head. "You'd think he could have got the drive the right width in the first place. I mean, it was only built a few years ago and now they're widening it."

Red-haired Stephen Chuff grinned and said, "Makes more of a job, doesn't it? If he hadn't designed the drive too narrow it wouldn't have to be widened. So half those men would probably be on the dole. Like my brother."

"I though he was working at the pig farm?" said little Sue Eames.

"Not any more he's not," said Stephen. "They've put up new buildings with automatic mucking-out."

"I don't think an architect would do something like that on purpose, though," said Matt Aiken, trying to be fair. "I expect he had some idea that it would be safer to have a narrow drive. Force all the cars to go slowly or something."

"Well, we couldn't go any slower than we are now," put in Rachel cheerfully, "because we've stopped."

Danny was looking smug. "I think I'll be an architect," he said. "I'd have got the drive right."

Matt grinned at his small friend and said, "*You* can't even keep your shoes done up!"

"That's because I lost the laces," said Danny with dignity, and tucked an unravelling piece of wool back into his sleeve. He was, Matt thought, quite the most untidy person he had ever seen.

The bus began to move again, nosing its way between wheelbarrows and cement mixers and stopping at last in the bus park. Matt and his friends got off and walked across the tarmac towards the dark-timbered, barn-like buildings of the school. Mr Potter, their form master, was fighting his way through the door with a bulging briefcase in one hand and a stack of books under the other arm.

"Oh, sir, you *are* in a muddle," scolded Rachel, opening the door for him. "Your glasses are all misted up and what *have* you done to your hair?"

"It's the wind," said Mr Potter, whose hair stuck up in erratic tufts. "And I'm late."

"But we're all late, too," said Matt reassuringly, "so it doesn't matter. They're digging the drive up and the buses can't get in. Well, only slowly."

"Absurd," said Mr Potter. "This place gets madder."

They all arrived together in the classroom with its high, sloping ceiling and red-painted girders. Everyone who didn't depend on the buses to get to school was already there, talking loudly. John Beasley was trying to juggle with two oranges.

"Quiet!" shouted Mr Potter, sliding his stack of books on to his desk. Nobody took much notice. The books slipped gently sideways and spread across the wooden surface, two or three falling over the edge. Peter Box retrieved them from the floor obligingly and said, "Haven't got it together this morning, sir, have you?"

"Leave him alone," scolded Rachel. "Mr Potter's lovely."

Mr Potter wiped his glasses and ran his fingers through his hair, then bellowed, "Right! Shut up, you lot, and sit down quickly. I've got a bit of news for you."

When everyone was more or less sitting down Rachel said, "Go on, then, sir—tell us!"

"Not until everyone's listening," said Mr Potter. "John, put those oranges away."

"One of them's mine," said Peter. "Ergh! He's made it all squishy."

"Doesn't matter," said Rachel crossly. "I want to know what the news is. Go on, sir."

Mr Potter waited until everyone was quiet. Then he said, "As you know, our Parents' Association have been beavering away making money for us—fêtes and barn dances and I don't know what—and at the end of last term they'd collected a good bit and we had to decide what to spend it on."

There were a number of shouted suggestions and Mr Potter held up his hand for silence. "We've done the choosing bit," he said. "Anyone who's not solid Plasticine between the ears might remember we had a ballot last term. It was decided that we'd buy a video tape recorder."

"We got one of them at home," said John Beasley. "I seen 'Superman' fourteen times. Cor, smashing!"

"*If* I may continue," went on Mr Potter, glaring at him. "Due to a generous discount at a shop run by one of the parents we had quite a lot of money left over after we'd bought the VTR. Mr Hazzard found that if we scraped the bottom of the School Fund bucket and put it with the left-over money, we'd have enough to buy something else. Something that makes the VTR doubly valuable to us."

He paused impressively, and Rachel shouted, "Yes, but *what*?"

"A television camera," said Mr Potter, smiling.

Instant hubbub broke loose. There were shouts of, "Lights!" "Music!" and various imitations of clapper-boards. Rachel broke into a chorus of "They're Gonna Make a Big Star Out of Me!" Marcia rolled her black mascara'd eyes and gave a whistle of derision at her friend's performance.

"Quiet!" bawled Mr Potter. When some order was restored he went on, "Look, stop all this mucking about or it'll be time for Assembly and I won't have told you anything about it."

"Go on, sir," said Rachel earnestly. "We'll be good."

"The point is," said Mr Potter, "this camera enables us to make our own video tapes. It can provide us with a record of anything we do in the school which we think is worth seeing again later—shows, sports days, camping, that sort of thing—but Mr Hazzard is very keen on using it more creatively. He feels that now we've got a camera of our own, we ought to be able to find out at first hand exactly what it's like to make a proper television programme."

"Can we do commercials?" asked John Beasley, provoking an outbreak of chanted advertising slogans and jingles.

"No, we can't," said Mr Potter firmly. Amid groans, he went on, "This isn't just a toy. It's a *very* expensive piece of equipment and it's got to be used sensibly. Now, what Mr Hazzard suggests is this. First of all, everyone should say what they personally would most like to do as the first project for the VTR and camera. As always, our headmaster takes a democratic view, Heaven help us. So I want you all to think seriously about it. Try and decide what is the best use for this new equipment. Bear in mind that the aim should be to make something we can keep in the school as a permanent record of what you people chose to do."

"Music hall," said Rachel.

Mr Potter blinked. "I beg your pardon?"

"Music hall," Rachel said again, firmly. "Everyone can do their own thing. People who learn ballet can dance, John can juggle oranges, Danny can tell funny stories, and I'll do 'Father, Dear Father, Come Home'. In a white pinny, with a candlestick."

Amid a chorus of groans, Mr Potter said encouragingly, "Well, it's a perfectly sensible suggesion. Write it down, Rachel, with your name and form on it, and I'll make sure Mr Hazzard sees it. You can spell 'music hall', can you?"

"Oh, get off," said Rachel. "I'm not *that* awful."

"I'm not so sure," said Mr Potter. "I still haven't got over the time you wrote, 'He pused open the door and draged out the man who was siting at the table.'"

"Well, you knew what it *meant*," said Rachel.

Mr Potter took a packet of exercise paper out of his desk drawer and handed it to Matt. "Give out one sheet each, please, Matt. Name and form at the top, everyone. Meanwhile, are there any other good ideas?"

"Wildlife," said Stephen.

Bill North snorted and said, "Don't be daft. You have to have special telephoto lenses and things. And go to Africa."

"There's wildlife in Britain," objected Sue Eames. "We've got a hedgehog in our garden. And my sister's got a gerbil."

"Gerbils aren't wildlife," said Peter Box.

"Put it down as a suggestion," said Mr Potter firmly. "We can talk about the nitty-gritty afterwards. Any other ideas?"

"Superman," said John Beasley.

"Been done, you twit," said Danny.

"We could have a space capsule going to the moon," Michael Chalmers suggested, "and it gets attacked by aliens and—"

"How d'you think we're going to do all that?" demanded Marcia, whose beetroot-red hair stuck out all over her head like a huge dishmop. "Costs thousands, dunnit? You want a proper studio and a scene dock and electronics and—I mean, we're not blooming Hollywood, are we?"

"Well, you think of something, then," said Michael huffily.

Marcia shrugged. "Nothing to do with me," she said. "Do what they like, can't they."

Nobody took any notice. Marcia had caused some consternation when she first arrived, but everyone was used to her now. "You can be in the music hall," Rachel said to her. "Wearing fishnet tights, standing against a board to have knives thrown at you."

"What, by one of these?" cried Marcia, indicating the boys in the class. "You got to be joking."

"We're not getting *on*," fretted Mr Potter. "It's no good trying to be democratic if people don't do their bit. Now, by tomorrow I want everyone to write a reasonable suggestion on their piece of paper and hand it back to me."

"I like it when they have all these people in the studio and throw custard pies at them," said John.

"Great!" agreed Peter Box. "How do you spell 'custard'?"

"Don't ask me," said Rachel gloomily.

The bell rang a double peal for Assembly and everyone stood up noisily. Matt, sitting near the front, caught Mr Potter's eye and grinned with some sympathy. Mr Potter ran his fingers through his dishevelled hair and said, "The things we let ourselves in for." Then he took a step back and shouted, "Right! Line up by the door. And *no talking!*"

The first lesson after Assembly was Science. Everyone was talking loudly about their television ideas as they wandered into the chemistry lab and dumped their bags on the benches.

"I think we ought to do some sort of documentary," said Matt.

"Boring," said Felicity.

"I don't know," said Rachel thoughtfully. "It might be quite fun. I wouldn't mind being Our Own Reporter, going round asking awkward questions." She thrust an imaginary microphone under an imaginary nose and said, "Excuse me, Mr Watts, but have you found your extreme unpopularity in the school any handicap to your career as a teacher?"

Danny, supplying the part of Mr Watts, the Senior Master, answered in an outraged bellow, "I *beg* your pardon? Take a million lines!"

"And two years' detention," added Peter Box gloomily.

"Perhaps it wouldn't be fun, after all," said Rachel.

"But a documentary would be easiest," said Matt. "You don't have to write a story or paint scenery or have actors. You just go out and film what there is. But then, I quite like painting scenery," he added reflectively.

The lab technician came out of his little room and approached them angrily. He wore a starched white coat of icy stiffness and his fair hair was cut very short.

"You will please be taking these things off the benches," he ordered. His pale blue eyes glared through his rimless glasses and his foreign accent was impossible to ignore. Everyone giggled.

"Okay, Fritz," said Michael Chalmers.

"*Kritz,*" corrected the technician furiously. "And you should be saying, *Mr* Kritz." He gestured angrily at the benches. "What is the use of putting out the equipment on the benches if you are also putting the bags on the benches?"

"What equipment?" asked Felicity innocently.

"Each station is having a bunsen burner, a small dish, a tripod and a wire gauze," said Kritz righteously.

"Big deal," said Debbie Smart.

"No need to get his knickers in a twist," muttered Marcia.

"I shouldn't think he could," said Rachel acidly. "They're probably starched."

"That bloke's really creepy," said Felicity, as Kritz continued to fuss over the removal of the bags. "He's like the baddie out of a horror film. He gives me the absolute heebies."

"I don't think he likes people in his lab at all," said Matt. "He wants the whole place completely clean and tidy—and empty."

At that moment Mr Dodds, the Chemistry master, came in, followed by a young woman in a white coat whom nobody had seen before. She had fair hair worn in plaits round her head and her brown eyes bulged slightly in a small-chinned face with projecting front teeth. She looked very much like a frightened rabbit.

"Cor," said John Beasley in gleeful anticipation, "is she going to teach us, d'you think?"

"Hope so," said Michael, rubbing his hands. "This'll be a laugh."

"Sit down quickly," said Mr Dodds impatiently, hands thrust into the pockets of his dilapidated white coat. "Oh, come on, come on, I haven't got all day." When the class was quiet he went on, "Now, this is Miss Plumforth, who will be in the school every Monday for the rest of the term. She will be teaching you for the next few weeks, and I expect everyone to remember their manners." He glared round for a few moments then smiled at Miss Plumforth and went on, "I must say, I'm delighted to have some help in the department, overworked and underpaid as we all are." She smiled nervously back. "Would you like me to stay for a while?" he asked politely, "or will you be all right? Mr Kritz will be at hand to supply you with anything you need."

Kritz bowed stiffly and everyone giggled again.

"Creepy," whispered Rachel, nodding at Felicity.

"I'll be all right," said Miss Plumforth bravely, and Mr Dodds said, "Good. In that case I'll get on with a few things. I'll be in the staff room if you want me."

"Doing the crossword," muttered Danny.

When Mr Dodds had gone out Miss Plumforth said, "Now, I expect you've all done some preliminary work on combustion, have you?"

"You what?" said John Beasley blankly.

"Burning, you twit," said Peter Box. "Here, Miss, are you a student?"

"Actually, yes," said Miss Plumforth, blushing slightly. "Now, today we're going to do some work on the various substances contained in crude oil, testing their combustibility. I thought you'd enjoy this—most children like messing about with things like oil, don't they?"

"I don't" said Felicity at once. "It gets all over your hands and it's yukky."

"Don't have to do it if you don't want," Marcia advised her. There were general nods among the girls, and Debbie said, "We don't *have* to, Miss, do we?"

"Yes, I'm afraid you do," said Miss Plumforth, turning pinker. "There's no need for you to get it on your hands—you'll only be dealing with a small amount in a test tube. Do be quiet," she added to the boys at the back, who were talking loudly and flicking bits of paper at each other. She returned her attention to Debbie, adding, "Anyway, for at least half the lesson you'll be writing notes."

Michael Chalmers raised a languid hand and said "Forgot my notebook. Can I go and get it?"

"You don't want to let him out, Miss," warned Felicity, taking pity on the student. "He'll be ages, messing about in the bog."

"No, I won't!" protested Michael. "Just want me notebook, don't I?"

"Well, be quick," said Miss Plumforth weakly.

With a grin and a wink, Michael went out.

"The rest of you, get your books out," ordered Miss Plumforth, "and ball-point pens for writing and pencils for diagrams."

"I'm awful at diagrams," said Debbie chattily. "Anyone got one of those stencil things?"

"Do please be quiet!" shouted Miss Plumforth against the rising tide of noise. Nobody took any notice. "Quiet!" she shouted again. "I want to tell you what we're going to do!"

The door opened and Mr Watts flung Michael Chalmers into the room by his collar. "We don't have people wandering round the corridors," he barked. "Asking for trouble."

An instant hush had fallen on the lab and the Senior Master glared round, taking in Miss Plumforth's flushed and pathetically pop-eyed face as he did so. Then he returned his attention to the class. "I don't think there's any need to say anything to you lot," he ground out with menace, "but I should like to know, Miss Plumforth, of anyone who causes any bother." He added quietly, "If you write a name down, get it off the front of the kid's work book. Don't believe what they tell you." With a last threatening stare round the room, he went out and shut the door.

"Crude oil," said Miss Plumforth quickly, in the quiet which Mr Watts had caused, "is the basic substance from which we derive a number of inflammable products in daily use. Can anyone suggest some of them?"

"Chip fat," said John.

Miss Plumforth smiled. "Actually, no," she said. "Any kind of oil you eat has to be derived from a vegetable or animal source."

"My mum set a chip pan alight once," said Sue Eames. "It was ever so frightening. And the ceiling was all black afterwards. Dad had to redecorate the whole kitchen."

"You ever put an old tyre on a bonfire?" asked Peter. "Talk about pong!"

"Do be *quiet*!" said Miss Plumforth desperately. "What other products come from crude oil?"

"He wouldn't let me get my notebook," complained Michael, indicating the departed Mr Watts.

"Well, use a bit of paper, then," said Rachel impatiently.

Marcia shifted her chewing gum to the other side of her mouth and surveyed Miss Plumforth with contempt. "Don't know why she don't get on with it," she observed.

Miss Plumforth took a deep breath. "Bring your stools up to this bench," she instructed, "and I will demonstrate the procedure for this experiment."

Noisily, everyone did as she asked. There was growing delight as she showed them the various inflammable substances present in crude oil, with much furtive nudging and grinning as the possibilities for sabotage became evident. Rachel said quietly, "She must want her head read," and Matt, overhearing, nodded in agreement. This lesson was going to be bedlam.

Miss Plumforth was neat and quick, showing them how a small quantity of crude oil could be split into its component parts in exactly the same way as a refinery carried out the process, but only about half the class could hear what she was saying. John Beasley's watch played a non-stop performance of "Greensleeves" in a high-pitched chirp, and soon every other digital watch in the room had joined in with a variety of pings and bleeps.

At last Miss Plumforth said loudly, "Right! I will ask Mr Kritz to give out the test tubes of crude oil. Everyone back to your places now."

Amid the clattering of stools being taken back to the benches. Matt saw Kritz approach Miss Plumforth and say something to her. She nodded. "Listen!" she shouted to the class. "Nobody is getting the materials to begin this experiment until Mr Kritz can see that you are sitting down quietly and being sensible."

"Don't know why *he's* got to stick his oar in," grumbled Peter Box. "Nothing to do with him, is it?"

"Doesn't want his lab messed up," said Stephen.

Rachel said righteously, "Mr Dodds oughtn't to go off and leave her like that, poor thing. It's a shame." But even as she said it, Matt noticed that her eyes were sparkling with an unholy enjoyment of the chaos. Kritz was reluctantly distributing test tubes containing a measured quantity of thick, black oil and within a few minutes the stuff seemed to be everywhere. Bunsen burners flared and smoked and there were shrieks of protests as various unorthodox things were subjected to a combustion test.

"Oy!" shouted Peter Box, rescuing his notebook from Michael Chalmers, "Burn your own blooming notebook!" He dowsed its smoking cover under the tap.

"Haven't got it, have I?" said Michael, aggrieved.

A terrible smell arose as Stephen found a chicken feather in his pocket and put it in the Bunsen flame. John Beasley, his face streaked with crude oil, was doing an imitation of some Zulu warriors he had seen on television and there was a crash as someone else's test tube landed on the floor.

"They make you do some blooming silly things at school, don't they?" said Marcia to Rachel. "I mean, if you want to know what's in crude oil you can look it up."

Rachel shrugged. "I suppose they think you remember it better if you actually do it," she said. She could not resist a grin. "It's certainly more fun!" she added.

Sheets of smoky flame shot up from the back of the class as John managed to ignite his oil-soaked Science notebook. Several of the girls screamed, and Miss Plumforth hurried towards the outbreak—but Kritz was there first. He snatched up a grey-painted metal wastepaper bin and up-ended it over the blazing notebook.

"You," he snapped at John, "stand over there by the wall. And you two also." This was at Peter Box and Michael Chalmers, who opened their mouths to protest, then, seeing the icy fury in the lab technician's pale eyes, decided against it. Kritz grabbed a fire extinguisher from its clip on the wall and, shaking it, approached the inverted bin. Wisps of smoke curled from under its edges, and as he knocked it on its side with his elbow flames shot up again. A jet of foam from the extinguisher killed the small fire very quickly and when it was out Kritz put the blackened bin on the floor and pitched the empty extinguisher into it. Then he went across to the sink and washed his hands. There was dead silence in the room.

Miss Plumforth looked at Kritz unhappily and said, "Thank you." Her voice sounded shaky.

Kritz nodded in acknowledgement of her thanks. He dried his hands on a mauve paper towel, staring at the class. "So," he said. "You are calling yourselfs the kind-hearted English. Loving the dogs, loving the children. This lady is doing nothing to harm you but you are behaving like savages."

Several people smothered giggles and even Matt had to look down to hide a grin. He knew what Kritz meant but his way of expressing it was hopelessly funny.

"It was only a laugh," protested John Beasley from his position by the wall. Kritz advanced upon him and John shrank, but the technician merely shook the crumpled paper towel under the boy's nose and said, "You should be watching out, yes? Or I am having *more* to tell Mr Watts."

John said, "Flippin' 'eck," then subsided into silence.

"I'm sure they're all sensible people really," said Miss Plumforth, but nobody answered. Kritz, staring angrily at the mess of blackened paper and foam on the bench which had been so spotless an hour ago, muttered something inaudible. It was perfectly clear what he meant.

CHAPTER 2

Miss Plumforth Blows Up

At registration time a day or two later, Mr Potter said, "It seems the school has made up its mind about what to do with the television camera."

"Go on?" said Peter Box, interested.

"What?" demanded Rachel.

"By far the biggest vote," said Mr Potter, "was for some sort of documentary programme." There were some groans but he went on, "And we had a very strong bid from the Sociology people in the fifth and sixth forms to do a kind of filmed social survey of the district where we live."

"Don't get it," said John.

"Don't have to," said Marcia flatly. "If the fifth and sixth forms is going to do it all, that leaves you out, dunnit?"

"No, of course it doesn't," said Mr Potter indignantly. "Mr Hazzard would never agree to anything like that. No, what we're going to do is make a documentary film about the school and its surroundings. What sort of place we live in, what people do, what kind of work they have."

"If any," said Stephen gloomily. His older brother, George, had still not been able to find another job.

Mr Potter nodded. "We'll include a bit on the number of unemployed people. What we're going to do is ask everyone to compile a kind of report, not filmed in the first instance, just a written report, perhaps with pictures or diagrams, on some little part of the district we live in. We're calling each one of these a study unit. Jargon, I know, but there it is. We seem to need it these days."

"But what *is* a study unit?" asked Matt. "A field or something?"

"That's up to you to choose," said Mr Potter. "The simplest study unit would be a single person, I suppose, and what he or she does. Or a household. Or it could be a shop or a farm or a factory, but those are more complicated. What we want you to do, you see, is find out all you can about your chosen study unit. Write down the name and address of the person you are studying—or people—and where they live, what the place looks like, what kind of area it's in, how the people live, what they do, where they do it. Interview the people concerned and write down what they say, note all the facts you can find out, take photographs perhaps, or draw pictures—compile a complete report."

"We don't have to do all this in our own time, do we?" asked Debbie, looking alarmed.

"No, of course not," said Mr Potter. "As long as we know exactly where you are going, we imagine all these interviews will take place in school time."

"You mean we can go out?" asked Sue, "instead of being stuck here in the classroom?"

"Well, yes," said Mr Potter cautiously, "a few at a time. Obviously it'll take most of this term to get these preliminary reports finished. When they're all in we'll choose a few of them to do in more depth. Those few will be a part of the documentary film, with TV-type interviews recorded on video tape."

"The best ones," said Sue, without hope of this including her.

"Not 'best' exactly," said Mr Potter. "What we'll try and do is get a variety of reports that cover the whole scene. No matter how good they are, we couldn't use a dozen reports that all cover the same thing—Flaxton Football Club or something."

"So if you want your report to be used for filming," said Rachel thoughtfully, "it's got to be about something nobody else has thought of."

"Ideally, yes," said Mr Potter.

"Can I do the shop where my mum works?" asked Debbie. A lot more people started to call out ideas and suggestions.

"Now, hang on!" Mr Potter shouted above the hubbub. "That brings me to another point." When quiet was restored he went on, "Mr Hazzard feels that the real benefit of the scheme will be in getting people to study something they don't already know about. In other words, we don't want you to write a report about your *own* household or workplace—we want you to find out how other people live. And it ought to be as different as possible from your own life style. That's to say, if you live in a town you want to study something country-based. If you live in a village, your study unit should be a town one."

John Beasley shook his head. "Think I'd rather watch 'Superman'," he said.

"It's quite simple," Mr Potter persisted encouragingly. "What you do is, arrange between yourselves to do a swop. If you live in a town and you've got a friend who lives in the country, then you study each other. Try to notice any ways in which you are different." He opened his briefcase and took out a sheaf of forms, which he held up. "These forms are headed, 'Proposed study unit'. Underneath that there's a space where you fill in the name and address of the people you propose to study. We'll check, of course, to make sure no unfortunate soul is going to be studied by about fifty

Mill Greeners all at the same time. Yes, Rachel, what is it?"

"Does it have to be someone at the school?" asked Rachel, with a gleam in her eye.

"No, if you have something else in mind, so much the better," said Mr Potter. Then he thought of something. "Oh, one last thing. Very important, this, so listen. Before any study actually starts, you must check that your intended study-person doesn't mind. That's to say, once we've agreed that your idea for a study unit is a good one, the first thing you must do is go and ask the people concerned whether they are agreeable. You absolutely *mustn't* go poking round anyone's property without permission. If it's a farm or a factory it could actually be dangerous. You must have the owner's agreement and you must obey any rules he stipulates about when you can come and what you can see."

"Dead right," muttered Bill North, whose father was a farmer. "End up down the slurry pit else."

Rachel was beaming. "I think it's a lovely idea!" she declared.

"You would," said Matt. The thought of knocking on a strange door and asking the people who lived there all kinds of personal questions made him blush from his floppy fair hair to his toes, which curled with embarrassment inside his blue-and-white trainers.

At break time Matt and his friends went out to the paved area where benches and red-painted litter bins were provided among groups of berry-covered shrubs.

"I know just what I'm going to do," said Rachel excitedly. "There's an old lady called Mrs Jessup who lives in a bungalow near the primary school in Tavenham. I've been there with my mother to take Meals on Wheels in the holidays, and Mrs Jessup's *lovely*. She used to be a music hall artiste—you know, song and dance. She's got heaps of photos of her when she was young, and lots of them are with really famous people like the Lupinos."

"Who?" asked Danny.

Matt said, "So that's what gave you the idea of doing a music hall for the video thing."

"Partly, yes," admitted Rachel. "But if we've got to do this dull old documentary I'm going to study Mrs Jessup. She's more fun than a factory."

"I think a factory would be great," said Danny. "All belts going round and machines clanking and banging." He went into a one-man impersonation of a factory, waving his frayed sleeves in sweeping circles and making machine-type noises.

A passing fouth-year boy cuffed him over the back of the head and said, "Off your blooming rocker."

"You can just shut up, Terry Skinner," Marcia shouted after him. "You never had no rocker to be off of in the first place!"

Terry turned and came back, his hands thrust into the pockets of his much-scrawled-on denim jacket. "Oh, yeah?" he said, sticking out his chin. He was a very big boy, with his sandy hair cut in a half-hearted Mohican style, almost bald at the sides but with a crest of longer hair down the centre of his head.

"Yeah," said Marcia, unintimidated. She smiled coolly and added. "Reckon I'll do you for my social survey effort. Next best thing to wildlife, you are. Blooming apeman."

"If you wasn't a girl I'd flatten you," snarled Terry. He reached past Marcia and grabbed the packet of peppermints which Matt was offering to Danny.

"Here!" protested Matt, "give those back!"

"Get stuffed," said Terry. He helped himself to a

peppermint then turned and hurled the rest of the packet away across the paved area where it disappeared among some shrubs. Danny pelted after it.

"You *beast*!" shouted Rachel, clenching her fists. Terry leered at her. "Yeah," he agreed. "'Swhat you expect of an apeman, innit?" Then he spotted a friend strolling across the distant bus park and shouted, "Oy, Rich! 'Ang about!" He ran to catch him up.

"I wonder what *he'll* do for the social survey," said Matt, staring after Terry as Danny came panting back with the rather muddy packet of peppermints.

"Nothing," said Rachel contemptuously. "People like him never do anything about anything."

"Don't blame him really," said Marcia, as they came to a bench and sat down on it in the autumn sunshine. "It's a blooming silly idea. Who's going to want a lot of kids asking cheeky questions about how much you earn and that?"

"Oh, go *on*," said Rachel. "It's better than sitting in a classroom for hours on end. I think it's great, the way Mr Hazzard tries to think of interesting things."

"If you say he's lovely," Marcia warned her, "I shall scream."

"Don't!" said Danny, covering his ears and, for some reason, shutting his eyes as well.

"It's all right," promised Rachel. "I won't say it. But he is," she added quickly. Danny took to his heels—but luckily the bell went at that moment for the next two lessons before lunch.

In the following days Matt began to suspect that Mr Potter shared his own misgivings about the social survey. As the forms were handed back giving details of everyone's proposed study unit, Mr Potter gazed at them dubiously. "An awful lot of you have put down

'Farm'," he said. "Have you checked that you actually *can* go to a farm?"

"They all want to come to ours," said Bill North gloomily. "And it's not on. Dad says he can't be doing with it."

"I don't blame him," said Mr Potter. "Matt, you don't seem to have filled in a form at all. Neither have you, Bill."

"I just can't think of anything," said Matt. He wished there was some way to get out of the whole idea.

"Oh," said Mr Potter. "What about you, Bill?"

Bill hunched his solid shoulders in some embarrassment. "Matter of fact," he said, "I just don't fancy it."

Mr Potter thought for a minute. "I can see what you mean," he admitted. "But what can I say? It's something everyone's meant to have a go at." He was struck by an idea. "Tell you what—why don't you do each other? You share the same reluctance, so perhaps it would work out quite well. You wouldn't tread on each other's toes, so to speak."

Bill and Matt eyed each other with some sympathy. They were not unalike to look at, both round-faced and stockily built, except that where Matt's hair was fair and floppy, Bill's was brownish, cut very short as if he couldn't be bothered with it.

"I suppose Mum wouldn't mind," said Matt. "What about your dad, though? You said he couldn't be doing with it."

"If it's just a friend of mine it's different," said Bill. "He'd never object to me having a friend round. He just doesn't like people interfering."

"I don't blame him," said Mr Potter again. He ran his fingers through his spiky hair, looking more worried than ever. "We plunged into this idea too quickly," he said. "You really will have to be very careful how you go about it, you know. People don't like being asked personal questions."

"What's a personal question?" asked Michael. Several people groaned at his ignorance and Mr Potter said, "Well, about how much they earn, for instance. Most people regard anything to do with money as their own affair."

"You know the bottle factory behind the station?" said Danny suddenly. "Well, I went round there to ask if I could do it as my study unit and the bloke was really nasty. He told me to—er—shove off."

"Oh, dear," said Mr Potter.

"Well, I don't care what anyone says," Rachel declared firmly. "I think it's—"

"Lovely," they all chorused.

Rachel looked offended. "Actually," she said with dignity, "I was simply going to say that it's a super idea and I think people ought to stop moaning and get on with it."

Mr Potter shook his head and smiled, but he still didn't look happy.

As the days went past the school seemed to divide itself into those who were enjoying the social survey and those who were not. Danny, who had managed to fix a visit to a bread factory, was full of good cheer and so was Debbie, who had arranged to study a hairdresser. Stephen said he was going to see a butcher in Flaxton (neglecting to mention that the butcher was his uncle), and Peter Box, who did a paper round before school, announced that he was studying someone who did a paper round. Matt and Bill were still very gloomy about the whole business despite their agreement to exchange visits to each other, but Rachel was full of enthusiasm for her plan to interview old Mrs Jessup.

Felicity couldn't make up her mind. When they all went into the lab on the Monday morning following Miss Plumforth's disastrous lesson on crude oil, she looked thoughtfully at Kritz, who came past carrying a rack of jingling test tubes. "Where do you live, Mr Kritz?" she asked innocently.

The lab technician stopped and stared at her. "What is that having to do with you?" he asked.

"I just wondered if you were a good contrast," Felicity explained airily. "If your life style was very different from ours."

Matt thought Kritz was going to explode. The man's face flushed an angry pink as he shot a furious look round the cheerfully gossiping class. Felicity realised that she had blundered and said hastily. "It's for the social survey, you see. We've all got to find a study subject."

"You people, you all going crazy?" demanded Kritz. "What next is happening? When you are finish with your spying, next what comes? The Gestapo? The knock on the door in the night, the taking away people who are not liking the social survey?" The test tubes chattered on their wooden stalks as he shook a clenched fist to emphasize his point. "You think is funny?" he went on as one or two people grinned. "Listen, in my country I am qualifying as a doctor. Then comes a system that is not okay—no good for living civilised life, no freedom. I am coming to this country. Free, yes, very nice—but my qualifications? Pha!" He gave a dismissive sweep of his white-coated arm. "Not recognised. So I work here, like servant. But nobody ask questions, all right? Nobody!"

Miss Plumforth came in and looked startled to find the class so quiet. Kritz picked up his rack of test tubes and went into the preparation room.

"Bloke's a nutter," said Danny.

The momentary spell cast by Kritz was broken and imitations of his outburst were going on all over the room.

"Be quiet and sit down," said Miss Plumforth loudly. "All of you." Matt thought that she had probably been given some hints on class management by Mr Watts. She sounded much more determined.

"That's better," continued Miss Plumforth as some order was established. "Now, as a lot of you were very silly last week, we will not be doing any practical work today. We will use this lesson to write up our notes on the crude oil experiment."

"Aren't we going to burn nothing?" asked John Beasley.

Miss Plumforth stared at him. "I am surprised you have the cheek to suggest it," she said.

"We done lines," protested Michael.

"And detention," agreed Peter. "Mr Watts had us in on Wednesday."

"And my dad had to buy a new wastepaper bin," said John gloomily. "*And* a new Science notebook. He wasn't half fed up."

Miss Plumforth took a deep breath and started again. "As I just told you," she said, "this week everyone will draw a proper diagram of the apparatus and write complete notes on the work we did last week."

Amid grumbles, Rachel put up her hand.

"Yes?" asked Miss Plumforth warily.

"I've done all that," said Rachel. "Mr Dodds always makes us write up our notes for homework and I thought we might be having him this week, so I did it."

"So did I," chimed in Matt and Felicity and several others.

"Oh." Miss Plumforth was nonplussed. "Well, you

can hand in your books for marking and—er—do something sensible while the others catch up. Read or something."

"Can we play Hangman?" asked Debbie.

"No," said Miss Plumforth quickly. "No, definitely not."

"All right," said Marcia, "keep your hair on."

There was general laughter. The noise was getting louder.

"We'll do our social survey," announced Stephen. "We've got to discuss it."

"Well—all right," Miss Plumforth conceded. "But quietly."

It was a mistake. All the people who had finished their notes considered themselves permitted to talk, and made the most of it. Most of the note-writers had no idea what last week's lesson was supposed to be about and certainly did not intend to write anything down if they could help it. Things got worse and worse. John and his friends were flicking chewed paper pellets about and turning on the water taps which, with a finger placed underneath, squirted a jet of water for some considerable distance. The growing number of people who had finished their work or decided they couldn't do it, gossiped and laughed loudly. Felicity got out her knitting.

Miss Plumforth stared in disbelief at the striped and shapeless woollen object which hung from Felicity's busy needles. "What *do* you think you are doing?" she demanded.

"Getting on with my leg-warmers," said Felicity comfortably. "I mean, there's nothing else to do, is there?"

"You do not *knit* at school," said Miss Plumforth. "You have a social survey project to get on with, so kindly get on with it."

Rachel smothered a slight yawn. "Actually," she said in a bored voice, "there's no point in talking about the social survey. It's all under control. We know what to do and we're doing it. But of course, you wouldn't understand about that."

The condescension in Rachel's voice was the last straw for Miss Plumforth. Her pop-eyed face flushed a bright red with fury as she clenched her fists by her sides as if to prevent herself from hitting the curly-haired girl. "*Actually*," she said to Rachel sarcastically, "cheeky little kids like you who think they know it all make me absolutely sick. Just because your parents have got more money than sense and choose to give the school a VTR and camera you go about behaving like Greta Garbo and Marlene Dietrich rolled into one. And none of you have the faintest idea what you are talking about. Your ideas on how to make a programme simply make me *laugh*."

Everyone was listening in appalled delight. "I'd like to take that equipment away from you lot," Miss Plumforth stormed on, "because it's absolutely wasted on you. At my college there are people on a full-time Film course who desperately need decent equipment, but they have to put up with old stuff because the college is short of money as always. They could show you what to do with your precious electronic toy. You have so *much*, you kids, and you just don't deserve it. You're just—just spoilt brats, all of you!"

Eyebrows were raised and several people whistled. "Ooh, nasty," said Marcia lightly. There was a roar of laughter.

"I'm a spoilt brat!" whined Peter Box in a babyish wail.

"*Spoilt brat!*" roared Michael like an outraged father, thumping Peter over the head. Peter gave a howl of pretended pain and sobbed theatrically.

The door opened and Mr Potter came in.

There was so much noise going on that nobody noticed him at first, then Rachel turned round from laughing at Peter, saw Mr Potter and gasped. She nudged Felicity who looked up, also gasped, and rammed her knitting away in her bag.

An uneasy silence fell. Mr Potter stared at them. At last he said, "I wouldn't have believed it. You got yourselves into trouble last week and I had words to say about it, didn't I?"

They nodded. Mr Potter turned to Miss Plumforth, who seemed a little out of breath. "I can only apologise on their behalf, Miss Plumforth," he said. "There are one or two people in this group who are known to be a bit silly on occasions but on the whole they're a pretty decent lot. Usually." He turned back to the class. "What you don't realise is, I try to stand up for you lot," he said. "When people tell me you've been behaving badly I always think they may be exaggerating a bit, or maybe it was just one or two of you. Not the whole lot. Well, we all make mistakes, don't we? And sticking up for you was a mistake. It just made me look a proper Charley. So thanks a bunch, that's all."

He looked really upset, Matt thought, staring at his form master with some concern.

With a threatening glare at the class, Mr Potter walked across to Miss Plumforth and said quietly, "Actually, what I came in for was to ask if I put a bunch of keys in your pigeon hole in the staff room by mistake. You've inherited old Price's pigeonhole next to mine. He left last term. I just wondered if you might have picked them up."

Miss Plumforth looked startled. "I didn't even know I'd got a pigeonhole," she said. "And I certainly haven't seen any keys."

"No," said Mr Potter gloomily. "I didn't think you would have. It was just a forlorn hope. I'm pretty sure I took them out of there before I went on duty."

People exchanged glances. No wonder Mr Potter looked a bit frantic.

Mr Potter pushed his hands into his jacket pocket and advanced to stare moodily at the class again. "The way I feel about you people at the moment," he said, "I don't really want to ask you for anything, let alone for help. But a bunch of keys has gone missing and it's important to get them back. So if anyone should see them please hand them in at once."

There were nods of agreement. Rachel put her hand up.

"Yes?" said Mr Potter, not sounding friendly.

"I just wondered if you had any idea whereabouts we should look," said Rachel very politely. "Where they were last seen."

"If I knew where they were last seen," said Mr Potter, "I would have gone there and found them. Do try to think before you start talking, Rachel."

"Bet someone's pinched 'em," John muttered to Peter.

Mr Potter did not hear what he said but the fact that he had dared to say anything at all was enough. "John Beasley, get outside at once!" he bellowed. He snatched the door open and John got off his stool and shuffled out, looking aggrieved.

"And the rest of you," said Mr Potter, glaring, "just remember I'll be up and down this corridor quite a lot for the rest of this lesson. You won't know when I'm there, but you can be pretty sure that if you make a noise, I'll hear you. And there will be *hell* to pay!"

He marched out and slammed the door behind him, and the sound of his upraised voice telling John Beasley what he thought of him ebbed slowly as he marched his victim off down the corridor.

Rachel raised an appalled eyebrow at Matt, who made a face back. It wasn't like Mr Potter to get into such a tizz. Very likely, Matt thought, he'd been on the carpet himself. If Mr Watts had found out that a bunch of keys had been lost, he'd have something to say about it. And how.

CHAPTER 3

A Burglary

"They're being awfully *slow* with this drive," Sue grumbled at the end of that day. The bus was crawling behind several others down the impeded carriageway. "I wanted to be home early today. It's my sister's birthday."

"Told you, they're spinning it out," said Stephen. "If you've got a job these days you make the most of it, don't you."

"How about your brother?" asked Matt. "Has he found another job yet?"

"George? No." Stephen shook his head. Then he added, "I told him to go and ask Bill's dad if he wanted another worker, but I don't know if he did."

"I didn't think Mr North kept pigs," said Danny.

"He doesn't," said Stephen, "but George'll do anything. Got to, haven't you? It's not like teachers—they're lucky, they never get the sack."

"I'm glad Mr Potter got his keys back," said Rachel. "Wasn't he in a state!"

"Serves him right," said Danny. "I mean, it's silly, isn't it, losing a bunch of keys that opens everything. What if the wrong sort of people got hold of a master key? They could open every door in the place."

"Well, they didn't," said Matt. "Ollie found them over by the shed where he keeps his lawn mower and things."

"Ollie Withett? You mean that assistant caretaker chap?" said Stephen, frowning. "I wouldn't trust him an inch. I mean, what could the keys be doing over there? Mr Potter doesn't go round by Ollie's shed when he's on duty. It's miles away, the other side of the pavilion. He just walks round the paved area and chucks the people out who smoke behind the bicycle sheds."

"I don't see what you're on about," said Rachel. "What does it matter where the keys were, so long as they've been returned? And anyway," she added on a different tack, "who *said* they were by Ollie's shed?"

"Ollie did," admitted Matt. "I met him coming through the main door with them when I was taking the register down to the office after dinner."

Rachel nodded, still looking suspicious. "He's a sort of friend of yours, isn't he?" she said.

"Sort of," said Matt.

Rachel stared out of the window. The bus had at last got clear of the school gates and was gathering speed as it headed down the road towards Tavenham. "Ollie Withett's a bit weird," she said. "All that shaggy hair and the way he says rude things to people."

"Ollie's all right," said Matt.

"You don't think he might have made it up, saying he found the keys over there?" asked Rachel, then glanced at Matt and added quickly, "Of course, it *might* be true."

"I told you, Ollie's all right," said Matt indignantly. "If he says the keys were by the shed then they *were* by the shed."

"Well, I don't think it was Mr Potter's fault," said Rachel equally hotly. "He gets in a bit of a muddle sometimes but he's not careless, not really. If he dropped his keys I bet someone else picked them up and kept them for a bit, then chucked them away near the shed."

"But why would they do that?" asked Danny, frowning. He was tugging at the zip of his anorak, which seemed to be stuck. "Why not hand them straight in?"

"*I* don't know," said Rachel crossly. "I'm just saying it wasn't Mr Potter's fault."

"Nobody's saying it was," said Sue. "I don't know why you're getting so het up. It's not as if any harm's been done."

"Is anyone any good at disentangling things?" asked Danny, looking up from his zip.

"What sort of things?" asked Rachel.

"Well, I seem to have got a bit of my sweater zipped in with my anorak," explained Danny, still tugging, "and when I tried to undo it because it's hot in this bus, it sort of undid my sweater as well. It's made a kind of hole and there's all bits of wool stuck in the zip. So I can't undo my anorak *or* do it up."

Everyone groaned. "Felicity's the knitting expert," said Rachel. "But she doesn't get on this bus."

In the effort to disentangle Danny, everyone forgot about the puzzle of the keys. At least, for the time being.

The following morning, there were two police cars drawn up in the small parking space outside Mr Hazzard's office.

"Look!" said Stephen, pointing towards the school as everyone got off the bus. A policeman was pushing his way through the shrubs which grew by the wall as he examined window catches.

"What's happened?" Matt wondered aloud.

"Been a burglary," said Stephen. "Must have been. He's looking for the way the thieves got in, isn't he?"

"I bet he's wasting his time," said Rachel darkly. "After that business with the keys yesterday, whoever broke in wouldn't have come through a window."

She was right. When Mr Potter came into the form room to call the register he looked grave. Everyone was quiet at once except John Beasley, whose watch chirped its idiot tune in the uneasy silence. Michael gave him a powerful nudge in the ribs and he switched it off.

"Bad news, I'm afraid," said Mr Potter, sitting down heavily. "The school was broken into last night. Well, not so much broken into as walked into. Whoever did it knew what they wanted and where to find it. They took the video tape recorder and the television camera. Among other things."

There was a general gasp of dismay.

"What do you mean, 'walked into'?" asked Rachel. "They had a key?"

"'Fraid so," said Mr Potter. "They didn't have to break any windows or force any locks."

There was a babble of discussion. "But, sir, if they've got a key they could come back and take other things!" said Danny.

"We're changing all the locks," said Mr Potter gloomily.

"How did they get a key?" asked John, and Michael nudged him again.

"He's so tactless," Rachel muttered to Matt, and Stephen leaned forward and asked, "When you saw Ollie with the keys, did he say there were any missing?"

"No," said Matt. "But he wouldn't know how many there were supposed to be, would he?"

"There weren't any missing," said Mr Potter, who had intercepted the question.

"Then how—" began Sue, but Marcia interrupted her. "Only got to have a key five minutes," she said, "then you can use it after."

Peter Box chimed in, "My dad says you can take an impression on a bit of soap."

"But you couldn't turn a bit of soap into a brand-new key and use it the same night," scoffed Rachel, then added doubtfully, "or could you?"

"Easy," said Marcia. "Any old key will do so long as it's the right kind of shape to start with. It's quite easy. Kids I was at school with in London did it all the time, some of them."

"Poor old Potter," muttered Stephen from behind Matt. "No wonder he looks sick."

"Where was the camera kept, sir?" asked Felicity.

Mr Potter looked at her. "I suppose there's no harm in you knowing, now that it's gone," he said. "In the cupboard next to the chemistry lab. Locked."

"But how did they know it was there?" asked Rachel.

Mr Potter shrugged. "No idea. Somebody told them, I suppose. It was no secret. All the senior forms know where the audio-visual stuff is kept. Was kept."

"Inside job, then," said Marcia.

"Mr Hazzard says he doesn't believe anyone in the school would do such a thing," said Mr Potter.

"Isn't that lovely," said Rachel sentimentally. "I do think Mr Hazzard's sweet."

"Daft, more like," said Marcia. "*Bound* to be an inside job, innit? Who else would know where the stuff was kept? What else did they take, sir?"

"Three cassette recorders and a reel-to-reel," said Mr Potter, "and a couple of projectors, one for film and one for slides. They didn't take the back projection unit that works like an epidiascope. No use to them, I suppose."

"They'd have needed some help with all that lot," Peter Box pointed out. "Too much to carry. Must have had a van or something."

"So it *wasn't* an inside job," said Rachel triumphantly. "Everyone's so horrid about Mr Hazzard, just because he tries to think the best of people. I think he's—"

"Yes, we know," interrupted Matt. "But, Rachel, if the stuff was pinched by people outside the school, they still had to know it was there. What's more, they had to know which cupboard it was kept in. So who told the thieves?"

A silence fell while everyone thought about this.

"A spy," said Rachel. "Somewhere in this school. One of us. What an absolutely horrible idea."

"Not one of us in this form," protested Danny, whose zipper-torn jersey now had a large new hole in the front, "because none of us knew where the stuff was, not until Felicity asked just now. It's got to be someone from one of the older forms."

"Or the staff," said Stephen.

"Yeah, what about the teachers?" said John Beasley, suddenly getting excited.

"Crawl back in your apple," Rachel told him.

There was an outbreak of excited discussion.

"Oh, shut up," said Mr Potter dispiritedly. "I just don't feel like a lot of noise today. And while I think of it," he added more severely, "I mean business about your treatment of poor Miss Plumforth. Any more of it and I shall really come the heavy. Give her a chance—you know she's only a student."

There was a mutter of reluctant assent.

"It's funny," said Felicity thoughtfully, "but some people—you just *want* to tease them, even if you're not really an unkind person. Do you know what I mean, sir?"

"I know what you mean," said Mr Potter cautiously, "but that doesn't make it any less unkind. A gang of thugs might say the same thing if they go into some little post office and rob the postmaster at gun-point."

"That's different," said Marcia firmly. "Little blokes in post offices are minding their own business. What

Fel means is, some people kind of stick themselves up—like as if they're asking for it. Specially teachers, 'cos they don't mind their own business. They're always trying to mind yours."

There were nods of agreement.

"I still say," persisted Mr Potter, "there are certain standards of kindness and decent behaviour, and you shouldn't let those standards down, whether to a teacher or anyone else."

"But *teachers* don't stick to those standards!" said Rachel indignantly. "I don't mean you, sir, but lots of them call us names and dish out all sorts of insults, much worse than anything we can say to them."

"Miss Plumforth said we were spoilt brats," Sue put in. "And she said nobody at this school had any idea how to use the camera and VTR. She said she'd like to take it away and give it to the people at her college who really needed it."

Mr Potter stared at her aghast, and Sue clapped her hand to her mouth as the full significance of what she had said came home to them all.

"So she did," said Rachel with interest. "And she could have got the keys, couldn't she? You asked her if she had them, didn't you, sir?"

"Creepy Kritz might have helped her," said Marcia. "*He* doesn't like the survey, either. He said it was like the Gestapo."

"That's quite enough!" said Mr Potter, jumping up and leaning his clenched fists on the desk. "I won't have you lot starting a stupid witch-hunt! People are free to express their opinions. Just because they say something a bit rash, it doesn't mean they're criminals!"

"And it doesn't mean they're *not* criminals," Marcia pointed out, staring at Mr Potter through her black-outlined eyes. "You can't be sure of anyone. Not *really* sure."

Mr Potter stared back at her for a few moments, then sat down abruptly and fished in his desk drawer for a red pen. "Time to call the register," he said. Then he remembered something. "Oh, Matt and Bill," he said. "You're both quite well ahead with your English and miles behind with the social survey, so if you want to use my English lesson last two periods this afternoon to catch up, you can do."

"We decided we'd study each other, like you said," Bill said cautiously.

"Yes, well, take yourselves off this afternoon and make a start," said Mr Potter impatiently. "Perhaps you'll get over this hang-up about it if you do something practical. All right?"

"All right," said Matt with some reluctance. Mr Potter was obviously in no mood to put up with any argument.

Bill North's farm was not far from the school, lying between Tavenham and the outskirts of Flaxton where Mill Green was sited. A footpath led to it across the fields, and Bill and Matt set off along this at ten to three, much to the envy of everyone else.

"Great to be going home early," said Bill. "Good old Potter."

"I'll have to go back and get the bus home," said Matt. "It's a heck of a long way round by road. Are you sure your dad doesn't mind me coming?"

"'Course he doesn't," said Bill. "Anyway, he won't see you. He's drilling turnips today—he can't possibly finish before tea-time."

As the boys came into the yard a black Alsatian dog appeared round the corner of the barn. It stood still for a moment, ears pricked enquiringly—then it came towards them in a silent rush, head down and an angry crest of fur standing up on its back. Matt instinctively ducked behind Bill. There was something unnerving about the dog's speed and the way it made no noise. As it charged towards them he heard that it was growling. The deep, rattling sound was amazingly menacing.

"Hello, Sarah!" called Bill. "Good girl, then!"

The dog came to a halt and looked sheepish, then began to wag her tail and whine ecstatically. There were white hairs round her muzzle, Matt noticed, and she had funny eyes. He looked more closely. "She's got one brown eye and one blue one!" he said.

"That's what you call a wall eye," said Bill. "She's getting old now and she can't see very well—I don't know if being wall-eyed has got anything to do with it. But you have to speak to her when you come in, so she knows who you are."

"She wouldn't attack you, would she?" asked Matt, alarmed.

"Oh, no," said Bill, "not once she knows you're a friend. But if you ever come here alone you'd be better to go through the front gate and ring the door bell. She can't get round to the front garden."

"I'll remember that," said Matt with feeling.

"What do you want to see first?" asked Bill, and Matt felt embarrassed again, remembering the purpose of his visit.

"I've no idea," he said. "I don't know anything about farms." He stared round. "It's very big and clean, isn't it? I thought there'd be hens running about, and lots of mud."

"It gets muddy in the winter," said Bill, "but we've had a dry autumn so far. I usually wear boots because if you go through the cattle yards wearing shoes, you get bits of straw in your socks. As to hens," he added, "we've got two thousand of them on deep litter."

"Where?" asked Matt, gazing round again. "I can't see any."

"Deep litter birds can't be *outside*, can they?" said Bill patiently.

Matt blushed and said, "Oh." He got his notebook out of his pocket and followed Bill as he set off on a guided tour of the farm buildings. Matt tried to make sense of Bill's stream of information about silage and stocking densities and conversion rates while Sarah sniffed under pallets in hopes of finding a rat, but most of the time he had no idea what Bill was talking about. He was quite glad of the diversion when a red Ford Escort estate car drew into the yard. The driver put his head out of the window and called, "Mr North about? My name's Parsons, from Silcox and Waggitt, agricultural chemicals. Had a message he wants to know about our new pre-emergence range."

"Oh, yes," said Bill. "I know he wants to see you. Quiet, Sarah!" he added to the growling dog. He turned back to the man. "Dad's out at the moment, I'm afraid. Can I help?"

The man got out of the car and said, "Could leave you the bumph, if you'd like to show him." A small knitted golliwog swung wildly on its string from the driving mirror as the man slammed the door shut and went round to the rear of the car.

Bill turned to Matt. "D'you mind?" he said apologetically. "Mum's out or she could deal with it. She does the Oxfam shop in the afternoons. I'll just get the chap to leave all the papers on Dad's desk and I'll be back. Oh—" he brightened. "There's Cyril. He's worked here for years. Ask him some questions—he knows all about everything."

Mr Parsons had retrieved a bulging briefcase from the car's tailgate, and Bill said briskly, "If you'd like to come this way." He led the man into the house with Sarah loping at their heels.

An enormous tractor had rumbled into the yard. The man who climbed down from the cab was lean and earthy-coloured, the eyes in his deeply-grooved face as wary as a fox's. He glanced briefly in Matt's direction then went into the barn. Matt, after a moment's hesitation, followed him. The man took a pitchfork from inside the door, spiked a bale of hay from the stack which rose to the church-like height of the barn's roof and turned to come out, almost falling over Matt.

"Sorry," said Matt. He trailed after the man called Cyril and watched as he let himself in through a gate into a yard where a lot of cattle turned their heads expectantly. Cyril pitched the bale effortlessly into a wooden hayrack then took a knife from his pocket, cut the bale's strings and pulled them free.

"Excuse me," said Matt as Cyril fastened the gate and trudged past him as if he was not there, "but could I ask you some questions?"

"You could try," said Cyril, going into the barn.

Matt gulped. What could he ask? Nothing personal. Nothing to do with money. "You work here?" he said desperately.

Cyril emerged with another bale. "What's it look like?" he said, opening the gate.

"Er—what time do you get here in the morning?" asked Matt wildly.

"Seven thirty," said Cyril.

"Oh. And you—er—feed the cows."

"Bullocks," said Cyril.

Matt tried again. "Does anyone else work here?" he enquired.

"One or two," said Cyril. Matt wrote it down. It looked silly. He racked his brains for a question which

Cyril would regard as more intelligent.

"Do you do the same jobs every day?" he asked, "or do you take turns with everything?"

Cyril was the far side of the hayrack, shaking the now-loose hay along the wooden slats as the black and white beasts crowded round him.

"I mean," Matt persisted as the man came out of the yard, "there's always someone here, is there? Or does everyone go and do things in the fields?"

Cyril stopped and looked at him. "What's it to do with you?" he asked.

"Nothing," said Matt wildly. "I mean, it's not for me, it's for the school. We're doing this social survey. We've all got to go and ask questions. Find things out."

"No wonder kids these days can't give you right change from a quid," said Cyril. "Be a darn sight better if you stuck to the three Rs."

He went back to the barn and stood his pitchfork in the corner. Matt trailed after him despairingly. "What are the three Rs?" he enquired without much hope.

"Reading, Riting and Rithmetic," said Cyril, setting off dismissively round the corner of a building.

"What are you going to do now?" Matt called after him, and then wished he hadn't.

Cyril, disappearing from view, did not answer, and Matt somehow could not bring himself to follow him. He stared at his rather crumpled notebook. On the open page he had written just two things, "Seven thirty" and, "One or two". It did not seem a very satisfactory interview, he thought. He was immensely relieved to see Bill and the man from the chemicals firm coming back into the yard.

CHAPTER 4

Sarah's Attack

Because the farm was within easy walking distance from the school, Bill North always went home for lunch. On the afternoon following Matt's visit, Bill came back rather late, bursting into the form room as Mr Potter was calling the register. "Guess what!" he said excitedly.

"Just a *minute*, Bill," said Mr Potter. He completed the list of names then looked at the unusually dishevelled and red-faced Bill. "Now," he said, "what is it?"

"Someone tried to break into our house!" said Bill. "Dad's furious!"

There was an instant outburst of questioning. "When?" "What happened?" "How do you know?"

"Mum had gone into Flaxton," said Bill, "to get a sack of calf milk powder and put in an order for Silcox and Waggitt. And Dad and the men were all out—they've started draining Three Mile Bottom, you see, so—"

"But did you catch him red-handed?" interrupted Rachel.

"No," said Bill. Then he grinned suddenly. "'Red-handed' is right, though! Or it was when Sarah had finished with him."

"Who's Sarah?" asked Sue.

"She's a dog," said Matt. He thought about the wall-eyed Alsatian with the grey muzzle and shivered slightly. He would not like to be alone in Bill's yard with Sarah.

"She doesn't like strangers," said Bill. "But I mean, that's what she's for, to be a guard dog. Anyway, when Mum came home, Sarah was standing outside the back door, growling like anything, and she didn't come when Mum called her. She seemed all upset. And when Mum went to see what was the matter with her, she found Sarah had blood all over her. Round her mouth and all down her chest and front legs."

"But she might have hurt herself," objected Stephen. "Are you sure it wasn't her own blood?"

Bill shook his head. "That's the first thing Mum did," he said, "stood Sarah on the kitchen table and looked her over carefully to see what she'd done. But she wasn't injured except for a lump on her ribs as if someone had kicked her. And when Mum looked in Sarah's mouth, she found she'd got a bit of material stuck between her teeth."

"Torn from someone's trousers," said Danny.

"Or jacket, perhaps," suggested Matt. "What colour was the stuff?"

"Black," said Bill. "Or perhaps dark navy—it was all wet, so you couldn't tell, really. But anyway, Mum could see Sarah had attacked someone, so she went outside to look round for any signs of people trying to break in."

"And?" prompted Rachel impatiently.

"They'd been at the kitchen window. There were dents all round the catch—really deep dents with the paint all chipped off—and Mum found a tyre lever on the ground, as if someone had dropped it. There was blood on that, too," he added with satisfaction. "The police took it away. They said it would have finger prints on it and they could check the bloodgroup, too. And they took the bit of stuff Mum found in Sarah's mouth."

Everyone was very impressed. "What were they after, do you suppose?" asked Danny.

"Can't be sure," said Bill. "Dad never keeps a lot of cash in the house—but he does have a lot of hi-fi stuff. He's a bit of a fanatic about it. His study looks like a recording studio."

"I know what's happened!" said Rachel. "Whoever took our camera and things must have had somebody to sell them to, right? A fence, they call it, don't they? Well, if this fence-person said, 'it's great stuff, everybody wants it, I can sell as much as you can lay hands on'—then they'd go and lay their hands on some more, wouldn't they?"

"But how would they know Bill's dad had got that sort of thing?" asked Felicity.

"Somebody told them," said Stephen. "Someone who'd been to the house and seen the stuff. Same as somebody told them what was in the cupboad beside the chemistry lab."

Bill was looking uncomfortable. "Matter of fact," he said, "Dad's coming to see Mr Hazzard about that."

"About what?" asked Marcia.

"Well—" Bill hesitated, then went on in a rush, "Cyril was grumbling about Matt asking questions yesterday for the survey. The trouble was, you were the second person he'd found in the yard that day, and he's a funny old chap about strangers."

"Who was the first?" asked Stephen.

Bill looked at him. "It was your brother," he said. "George."

"Oh, well, *that's* all right," said Stephen easily, "he was just looking for a job."

"I know," said Bill. "And I know Matt was just asking questions for the survey. But Cyril thought you were both poking about in what didn't concern you, and that's what he told Dad. And Dad's never liked strangers round the place."

Matt's face was scarlet to the roots of his fair hair. "But I never even went in the house!" he protested. It seemed to him that everyone was looking at him with a dreadful kind of interest.

"I know you didn't," agreed Bill. "And I don't suppose George did, either, but Dad won't listen. I really am sorry, Matt."

"Not your fault," Matt muttered.

Rachel said stoutly, "Well, it's up to us to find out who *is* the spy. We know it isn't Matt—"

"And it isn't George," said Stephen quickly.

"—and it isn't George," agreed Rachel, "so who is it? *Somebody* had to tell the thieves where our camera and things were kept, and *somebody* had to tell them about Bill's father's hi-fi stuff. All we've got to do is find out who it is."

"And the sooner the better," said Matt with feeling.

"Now just hang on a minute," said Mr Potter, who had listened for some time without interrupting. "This is all going much too far. It's not up to you to go hunting for spies. And as to the social survey—I rather think that's gone too far as well."

"Oh, *no*," said Rachel at once. "The social survey's *lovely*."

"I'm going to take my 'Superman' cassette to bed with me tonight," said John Beasley, who had been thinking deeply.

"Won't do you much good if they've pinched your VTR," said Marcia.

"Oh," said John. "No, that's right. Cor. Bad, innit?"

Matt glanced round the classroom and found that people were looking away rather than meet his eye. He tried to tell himself that they were sympathetic, really.

Nobody actually thought he could be the spy. Or did they? He opened his desk and delved about in it as if looking for a book. Somehow he didn't want to be looked at.

Danny slid across to the seat beside Matt and said, "You don't want to take any notice of that old bloke at the farm."

"'Course not," said Matt. He went on delving. Mr Potter was saying something rather tedious about social responsibility.

"Everyone knows it isn't you," said Danny.

Matt looked at his untidy friend unhappily and said, "Do they?"

Danny gave him a sudden, furious push as if to knock the silly idea out of him. Matt almost fell on the floor and books scattered in all directions. "Oh, all right," he said, laughing.

"Danny Williams, what *are* you doing?" said Mr Potter, exasperated. "We're trying to discuss something rather serious here and all you do is mess about."

Danny and Matt exchanged glances. "Sorry," said Danny meekly, and sat down with an expression of extreme virtue.

"Much as I approve of Mr Hazzard's policy of devising interesting projects," said Mr Potter, "I am inclined to have reservations about this one."

"You what?" asked John.

"He doesn't like it," Peter told him.

"I wouldn't go as far as that," said Mr Potter, "but I do think we are heading for trouble if we keep interfering in other people's business like this. I've never been quite happy about it, and the thought that it was by my instructions that Matt and Bill went—"

The bell rang its double peal.

"Oh, blast," said Mr Potter irritably. "There's never any time to *talk* to people in this place."

Matt was inclined to agree. But the next lesson was History, and Mrs Abbott was not tolerant of people who arrived late for her lessons.

Despite Mrs Abbott's eagle eye, Matt was struck by such a good idea during History that he could not resist writing a note to Bill North about it. Under cover of a propped-up textbook, he wrote, "What about the man from Silcox and Waggitt? You took him in the house." He folded the piece of paper and wrote Bill's name on the front then nudged Danny who sat next to him. Danny, not even looking at the note, continued to write as he passed it smoothly under cover of his desk to Debbie Smart, who made an equally professional job of passing it to Rachel. Rachel unfolded it to see what it said before passing it on. There was a gangway between her desk and Bill's, so she used the subterfuge of dropping her pen and picking it up as a cover for slipping the note across to Bill's feet. Mrs Abbott glanced up suspiciously but Bill was too sensible to pick the note up straight away. He covered it with his shoe and went on writing.

After a few moments of fierce scrutiny Mrs Abbott returned to the pile of books she was marking, while the class continued its notes on Early Canal Builders. Bill, scratching his ankle, retrieved Matt's note and risked a thoughtul nod in Matt's direction. Rachel meanwhile had been scribbling furiously on a page detached from the centre of her history notebook. Rachel's notebooks were always thinner than anyone else's because of the number of notes she wrote. Inch by inch, she pulled off the blank half of the double sheet of paper along its fold line and froze when Mrs Abbott looked up sharply again at the faint sound of tearing as Rachel's fingers moved too quickly. Rachel waited. Everyone sitting round her waited as well, knowing what was going on. Mrs Abbott's red pen began to move again—and so did Rachel, completing the detachment of the note then sliding it off her desk and into Debbie's waiting hand.

"*Right*," said Mrs Abbott. "I'll have that. Deborah Smart, come here."

Debbie stood up innocently and advanced, empty-handed.

Mrs Abbott sighed. "Bring the note with you," she said.

"Note?"

"Yes, note."

Debbie's courage failed. She retrieved the note from her chair seat and put it on Mrs Abbott's desk.

"Thank you," said Mrs Abbott. She glanced with distaste at both sides of the note, crumpled it and threw it into the wastepaper basket, then said in a bored voice, "Rachel Greenberg and Matthew Aiken, see me at the end of the lesson." Then she went on marking.

Matt groaned inwardly. This was not his day.

Rachel and Matt spent the afternoon break mending the covers of some dilapidated files with sticky tape, watched grimly by Mrs Abbott as she sipped a cup of tea. There was no chance of talking. Matt suspected that she kept the files exclusively for the purpose of providing a punishment task. They were far too battered for anybody actually to use.

Maths with Mr Watts was equally unsocial, so by the time Matt and Rachel were able to exchange a word school had ended and they were walking out to the bus park.

"What did your note say, anyway?" Matt asked.

"I just put, 'What man? Tell me more!'" said Rachel. "And a picture of me jumping up and down with,

'Excitement, excitement' written all round. Only I wasn't sure how to spell it. What did you mean in that note you sent to Bill?"

Matt explained about the agricultural representative who had driven into the yard in the red Escort when Matt was at the farm with Bill. "He looked perfectly respectable," he admitted, "wearing a cap and a checked jacket. But you never know, do you?"

"Of course you don't," agreed Rachel. "It could be anyone. The only thing is," she added thoughtfully, "a representative from a firm supplying farm chemicals isn't likely to know anything about our school, is he? Let alone where things are kept. But then, we don't *know* that whoever tried to break into Bill's house was after tape recorders and things. It might be quite separate."

"Yes," said Matt, beginning to feel rather silly. "I suppose I just grabbed the idea of proving it wasn't me."

Rachel laughed. "Don't be stupid!" she said. "Nobody thinks it's you. Sue thinks it might have something to do with Stephen's brother, though. He's got some pretty tough friends—all that lot who ride motorbikes. Most of them are on the dole, so they've got nothing to do all day."

Matt thought about it then said, "I hope it *isn't* George. It would be awful for Stephen."

"Yes," said Rachel. "I hope it isn't, too." Then she brightened up. "But there's one huge clue, isn't there—if Bill's dog bit somebody badly enough to cause all that blood, *somebody* is walking about with a great big bandage!"

"So they are!" said Matt. "I hadn't thought of that." Somehow, the idea cheered him up.

A car, parked near the cement mixer so as to be out of the way of the buses, began to hoot repeatedly. "It's

Mum!" said Matt, surprised. "What's she doing here?" He ran across to the car.

"See you tomorrow if you're getting a lift!" Rachel called after him.

"Okay!" Matt shouted back. He reached the car and said, "Hello."

His mother opened the passenger door. "Hop in," she said. "I had to do an extra stint at the library—Mrs Wadham had one of her headaches. So I thought I'd pick you up while I was still in Flaxton and get your hair cut before the school starts complaining. The hairdressers are so busy on Saturdays. They're always booked up."

Matt got into the car and shut the door. He hated having his hair cut. "Sometimes," he said, "I wish you'd never got a car."

His mother laughed. "You'd only have to go there on a bus," she said.

Half an hour later, with the inside of his collar prickling uncomfortably, Matt came out of the hairdresser's and met his mother outside Marks and Spencers as they had agreed.

"There," she said, "that wasn't so bad, was it?"

"It was awful," said Matt. The air felt cold behind his ears.

"Like a cup of coffee to warm you up?" offered his mother, trying to make amends. They were passing a steamy-windowed café with orange lights hung low amid a jungle of enormous house plants.

"I wouldn't mind," admitted Matt.

"Come on, then." They pushed open the door and went in.

"Over there, I should think," said Matt's mother, nodding towards one of the red-upholstered benches on the far side of the room. But Matt was standing as if transfixed, staring at a couple who sat at a table shadowed by the huge perforated leaves of a Swiss cheese plant. They sat hunched over the table with their heads close together, deep in discussion. There was a kind of privacy about them which seemed to exclude the outside world.

"Come *on*, Matt," said his mother from behind him. "Do move!"

"Sorry," said Matt. As he went towards the seat his mother had indicated he looked over his shoulder to make sure he had not mistaken the identity of the couple so engrossed in conversation. No, there was no doubt about it. They were Miss Plumforth and the angry foreign lab technician, Creepy Kritz.

As if aware of Matt's scrutiny, Kritz sat back and unfolded his arms. Their eyes met. And then Matt saw something which made the back of his neck prickle in a way which was not due to his recent haircut. The man's left hand was heavily swathed in bandages.

CHAPTER 5

Suspicions

"It *must* be him!" said Rachel excitedly. She was so thrilled by Matt's news about Miss Plumforth and Kritz and the bandaged hand that her curly hair seemed wilder than ever. "But what shall we *do*?"

It was break time the following morning and Matt and his friends were walking round the field, discussing the mystery of the Mill Green spy.

"There's nothing we *can* do," said Matt. "We can't be sure it's Kritz."

"In fact," Bill North said flatly, "it can't be."

"Why can't it?" demanded Rachel.

"Because the man Sarah went for was there at about half-past eleven or twelve o'clock," said Bill. "Just before Mum came back from Flaxton to get lunch ready. And Kritz would have been at school."

"Oh, blow," said Rachel, disappointed. "Why didn't I think of that? Now we've got to start all over again." She paced along moodily for a few minutes, her hands thrust into her cardigan pockets. Then she stopped. "The man Sarah went for," she said, struck by a new idea. "Perhaps it wasn't a man. It could have been a woman. Miss Plumforth is only at Mill Green on Mondays, isn't she?"

"Oh, yes!" said Felicity, suddenly understanding what Rachel meant.

Marcia took up the point as well. "You sure the bandage was on Creepy's hand, Matt?" she asked. "Some of these caffs is pretty dimly lit. It wasn't *her* that was bandaged, was it?"

For a moment Matt was tempted to delude himself that the bandage had been on Miss Plumforth's hand. It would fit in so nicely. But it wouldn't be true. He shook his head. "'Fraid not," he said.

"Bang goes another theory," said Rachel. "What a pity. But I'm sure it must be something to do with them. Hey—listen, how about this? What if Kritz and the man from the chemicals firm are friends? So the chemicals man was snooping at Bill's farm, and Kritz had told him about the video stuff here, and they both know somebody else who did the actual stealing! That's possible, isn't it?"

"I think it's boring," Danny said suddenly. "All this making up stories that might be true or might not—it's nearly as bad as English. I'm going to play handball." He ran off across the grass, followed by Stephen, who was notably reluctant to talk about the spy. Bill went as well and Matt was half inclined to follow him, but a glare from Rachel kept him where he was.

"They're such *kids*," said Rachel, staring with contempt at the boys, who were now hitting a tennis ball against the end wall of the school.

"I can see how they feel," said Matt. "Honestly, Rachel, do you really think anyone on the staff would be mixed up in something like this? I mean, *why?*"

Rachel stopped and turned to face him. Debbie and Felicity wandered on but Marcia stayed to listen, grinning. Little Sue Eames stood solidly at Rachel's side with her arms folded pugnaciously.

"Teachers are only human, same as the rest of us," said Rachel, "and they're not all that well paid. And Kritz is only a lab technician, so he gets even less, and as to Miss Plumforth—everyone knows how broke students are." Sue nodded loyally. "And anyway," Rachel went on, "there are other motives. A lot of people don't like Mr Hazzard's social survey, so the VTR and camera might have gone so as to nobble it. Kritz was in a real state about it, wasn't he? You can see he's got an absolute thing about people being persecuted. And look how upset Plum was about us having a television camera and VTR. She and Kritz are both nutty enough to pinch the stuff just to muck up the scheme—specially if they're in it together. And what else have they got to get together about in some café? They had to be up to *something*."

"Yes," admitted Matt. "They certainly looked like it. But there's lots of other people who don't like the scheme. Look at Mr Potter. He was going on about it yesterday."

"Mr Potter wouldn't dream of—" began Rachel, but Matt interrupted her. "How do you know he wouldn't? Just because you like Mr Potter you assume he can be ruled out as a suspect."

"*I* think he's a bit of a creep," said Marcia suddenly. "He wouldn't actually pinch the stuff—he hasn't got the bottle. But he might agree to just getting it out of the way for a bit until this survey thing has blown over."

"That's silly!" said Rachel.

"How do you know he didn't drop his keys on purpose?" demanded Marcia. "Be funny if the gear all turns up after a month or two, won't it?"

"But he couldn't," insisted Rachel. "I mean, he was really upset about losing his keys. And he kept on with the social survey, even if he wasn't very keen on it. I mean, he sent Matt off to Bill's farm, didn't he?"

Marcia looked pitying. "Got to put up a front, hasn't he?" she pointed out. Then she shrugged. "Maybe he didn't. I'm just saying he could have."

Rachel was looking quite upset. "Mr Potter would never do a thing like that," she declared. "I know he wouldn't. But it could be Stephen's brother. And what about that mad Ollie Withett? I know we stuck up for him when those fourth year boys tried to make out he'd set the school on fire, but that was different. I mean, he did find the keys. And what had he done with them before he handed them in?"

"You're just being silly," said Matt hotly. "I think I'll go and play handball." He turned away.

"And you're a suspect, too!" Rachel called after him. "Don't forget that!"

Annoyed though he was, Matt knew Rachel wouldn't say a thing like that if she really meant it, so he shouted back, "You're just jealous! You'd like to be a suspect yourself!"

"Yes, I would!" yelled Rachel. "I don't care what happens as long as it's exciting!"

Matt grinned to himself as he walked across the grass to the handball game. He couldn't help liking Rachel—but she was an idiot sometimes. He changed course to avoid some older boys who were walking across his path, but one of them reached out a hand and caught him by the hair. "Watch it," snarled the boy. It was Terry Skinner, with his friend Richard Walker and another boy whose name Matt didn't know.

"Ow!" said Matt, his eyes watering. "But I didn't—"

Terry gave him a push which sent him sprawling—then clapped a hand to his own ear and spun round, glaring. A tennis ball, expertly pitched by Danny, had hit him on the side of the head. The ball rolled towards Matt, who grabbed it, scrambled to his feet and ran to join the others.

"What about that for a shot!" called Danny, grinning. Then he took to his heels. A furious Terry was bearing down on him at full speed. Matt pelted after the older boy but was tripped up by Richard Walker's foot and fell headlong on the grass. He scrambled up again and saw Bill and Stephen try to head the fourth-year boy off—but to no avail. Catching up with Danny, Terry pushed the running small boy hard in the back. Danny was flung forward on to his hands and knees, skidding across the rough tarmac and rolling over until he sat up, clutching his knees. He was panting hard and Matt thought he looked as if he was trying not to cry. Danny's already rather threadbare grey trousers were torn across both legs, revealing deeply gouged knees from which blood was welling up. Gingerly, he inspected the palms of his hands which were also grazed and bleeding.

From a safe distance, Terry shouted, "Serve you right, you snotty little—" Then, seeing Mr Dodds approaching, he said no more but walked away with his friends, whistling innocently.

"Been in the wars?" enquired Mr Dodds as he came up to Danny. It was funny, Matt thought, how teachers never quite seemed to understand what was going on.

Danny nodded.

"Come on," Matt said, helping him to his feet. Stephen said, "It was that Terry Skinner, sir, he—"

"I don't want to hear any tales," said Mr Dodds. "Better get along to the medical room. No, come to think of it, there won't be anyone there at the moment. Come into the lab—I've got some first-aid stuff there."

"You shouldn't have thrown that tennis ball at him," said Matt to his small friend as he helped him along behind Mr Dodds. "But thanks all the same."

"Any time," said Danny grandly, though his eyes were watering.

Mr Dodds got a white-painted wooden box out of a cupboard and rummaged about in it. He found a floppy blue paper packet containing a rather small bit of cotton wool and looked at it crossly. "That's a fat lot of use," he said. He turned his head slightly and shouted, "Mr Kritz! What's happened to the first-aid stuff?"

Kritz appeared at the door of his room. The bandage on his hand had been replaced by a black fingerstall, tied at the wrist with tape. Somehow it made him look more creepy than ever, Matt thought.

"Ah," said Kritz. "Bandages. Yesterday I am having a small accident with my hand." He held up the black-sheathed finger. "There was much blood for which I was needing the cotton wool."

"Fair enough," said Mr Dodds, "but you could have replenished the box afterwards."

Kritz looked offended. "I was thinking it necessary for an anti-tetanus injection," he said. "I was causing the injury with breaking a glass tank in which are biological specimens living in earth. Tetanus, you are understanding, is—"

"Yes, I know all that," said Mr Dodds impatiently, "but—"

Kritz closed his eyes for a moment. "I was therefore going to the hospital straight away," he continued, "and was there remaining all my lunch hour as many people was waiting. The British medical services are not so clever, I am finding. On my return there was much work to do, and finding a new tank for the biological specimens."

"But you could have—" began Mr Dodds again.

Kritz had dived back into his room and came out with a new pack of cotton wool. "Simply, I am not yet putting it in the box," he said loftily. He nodded at Danny's injuries and asked, "You are wanting I am seeing to the boy?"

"No, you'd better go and have your lunch," said Mr Dodds rather irritably. "No sense in missing it two days running. I'll take care of this."

"As you are wishing," said Kritz haughtily.

When he had gone, Matt and Danny exchanged narrow-eyed glances. So Kritz had *not* been at school when the break-in at Bill's farm had been attempted! It could have been him.

"Just wait until Rachel hears about *that*," muttered Danny.

Mr Dodds handed Matt a white enamel basin and said, "Fill that half full with warm water, will you? May as well make yourself useful. Williams, hop up on the bench so I can see what I'm doing." And as Danny stiffly began to obey this instruction, Mr Dodds added, "You may as well take those trousers off. What's left of them."

"Well, that's it," said Rachel positivelv "It *must* have been him."

They were gathered in the form room for afternoon registration. "But how would Kritz know Mr North was keen on hi-fi stuff?" objected Felicity.

"I've been thinking about that!" said Rachel, with the air of one who has a trump card up her sleeve. "He looks after a chemistry lab, right? So he's bound to know the people who supply chemicals, isn't he? Perhaps the man Matt saw, who came to the farm about agricultural chemicals, is a friend of Kritz's. So when he went into the house with Bill he saw the stuff and let Creepy know."

"It's ingenious," said Stephen. "Rachel Sherlock Holmes-Greenberg does it again!"

Mr Potter came in and said, "Sit down quickly." He looked as if he had something to say, so everyone shuffled into their places and more or less stopped talking.

"Has my dad been up?" asked Bill. "He said he was coming today."

"He has indeed," said Mr Potter grimly. "And he's not the only one. We've had several complaints about you people asking questions—in fact, we've spent the whole dinner hour having a staff meeting about it."

"What did you decide?" asked Rachel.

"There was quite a lot of disagreement," said Mr Potter, "as you can probably imagine. Mr Hazzard feels that we went wrong in trying to get everyone involved—in making it compulsory. He says he thinks the people who are really interested are doing a good job and being sensible, making sure they don't upset anyone. Probably it's the people who don't want to do it who are causing the trouble—not on purpose," he went on quickly. "It could be just that they find the whole thing a bit difficult or embarrassing, so they tend to put their foot in it."

Matt nodded agreement.

"I done a survey," said John Beasley suddenly.

This was so unexpected that Mr Potter completely forgot what he was saying, "*Did* you, John?" he asked, sounding impressed. "What was that?"

"I done milk bottles," said John. "Like, Danny went down the bottling plant, didn't he? Only they slung him out. Well, I done how much milk people drink in our street. Counted the empties on the steps."

"What a sensible idea," said Mr Potter, amazed. "And how many were there?"

"Two," said John.

When the laughter subsided Michael said, "Told you not to do it after school. All been collected, haven't they?"

"Not my fault," said John.

Mr Potter shook his head. "All right," he said, "let's get on. The point is, we're cutting the scheme right down to just those who really want to do it. If you're not interested—okay, scrub it. If you are, you can still go ahead. But before you ask any more questions you must get the person you're interviewing to sign a form to say he or she doesn't mind. We're getting some forms duplicated this afternoon. That way we're all protected from any complaints and in the long run we'll probably get a better result—always supposing the police manage to find the VTR and camera, of course."

"Isn't that lovely!" said Rachel, ignoring the last part of what Mr Potter had said. "I call that really sensible of Mr Hazzard. Now those of us who want to do the survey have got a really good chance of getting our interviews filmed." She glanced at Matt and Danny and added, "*When* we get the camera back. There's no 'if' about it, is there!"

"Rachel, what are you up to?" demanded Mr Potter. "I don't want any more of your fancy ideas about people in this school being involved. Just leave it to the police. They'll sort it out in time."

"I want to sort it out *now*," muttered Rachel.

The first lesson of the afternoon was Music, which Mrs Gipsum had decided to devote to singing, "because," she said, "the sound produced in Assembly is a disgrace. Like half a dozen asthmatic starlings. Give out the hymn books, Debbie."

"What should we do about Kritz?" Rachel asked Matt as the hymn books were being distributed.

"Tell the police," said Matt. "Or shut up about it."

Rachel frowned. "I do wish we could really prove it," she said. "I mean, I'm sure he did it, and I think Plum's mixed up in it as well, but we're not absolutely *certain*. All we can say is that he *could* have done it."

"Rachel Greenberg, stop talking," said Mrs Gipsum. She had frizzy hair which reminded Matt of a poodle. Although she was rather fat she wore high-heeled shoes and walked in a bouncy way, and somehow that was rather like a poodle as well.

"'Ye Holy Angels Bright'," announced Mrs Gipsum, striking a chord on the piano. "Everyone runs out of breath at the end, so we're going to practise the last phrase. Listen." In a warbling soprano, she sang,

"For else the theme
Too high doth seem
For mortal tongue."

"Not a question of 'doth seem'," muttered Marcia. "It blooming well is."

"It just goes straight up the scale, you see," Mrs Gipsum explained, "with a little curly bit when it gets to 'for mortal tongue'. Listen while I play it."

"I'm glad we can go ahead with the survey, though," Rachel said to Matt as Mrs Gipsum turned back to the piano. "I thought they'd cancel the whole thing, specially after the camera and VTR were stolen."

"I expect they're insured," Matt pointed out. "So even if they never turn up, the school can replace them."

"Matthew Aiken, you sing it," commanded Mrs Gipsum from the piano stool. Matt blushed furiously. He was not sure if his voice would come out as a squeak or a croak. Either way it was going to sound dreadful. Mrs Gipsum thundered into the scale, and Matt emitted a series of strange sounds. Everyone laughed.

"Yes," said Mrs Gipsum. "No comment. Perhaps you won't talk in my lessons in future. Now, I'll play this at a lower pitch where you can all sing it easily, then we'll sing it a semitone higher each time. All together, now. For else the theme . . ."

Looking angelic, Rachel sang to the tune,

"I'm going to see
My old ladee
This wee—ee—kend."

She glanced at Matt as Mrs Gipsum played a couple of chords before the next chorus and said, "Why don't you come, too?"

Matt shot her a threatening glance. He didn't want any further involvement with the social survey—and what's more, he had no intention of risking another solo performance.

"No, honestly, you ought to come, Matt," said Rachel at break time. She pushed the door open and Matt followed her out into the paved area.

"Come where?" asked Matt.

"To see Mrs Jessup," said Rachel impatiently. "My old lady. Like I was saying in Music. I'll have to get her to sign this form."

"Look, we don't have to do the beastly survey now, if we don't want to," said Matt. "And I don't."

"Oh, not because of the survey," said Rachel. "That's why I'm asking you. If I thought you were going to muscle in on my study subject I'd keep Mrs Jessup to myself."

"Then why—" began Matt.

"I want someone to help me do a few practical things for her," said Rachel. "Chop some wood and screw a shelf back on to the wall where a bracket's come loose."

"Oh," said Matt. "You mean, I don't have to talk to her?"

"Don't be silly, Matt," said Rachel, exasperated. "You're talking to me, aren't you? And you don't mind that."

"Talking to a friend is different," said Matt. "It's not—official."

"Mrs Jessup doesn't want to be talked to *officially*!" cried Rachel. "She just enjoys people dropping in occasionally. And she could do with a few odd jobs being done. You'd like her, Matt—she's ever such an interesting person."

"M'm," said Matt, unconvinced. He thought about it, not noticing that Terry Skinner and his friends were idly approaching the bench where Matt and Rachel sat. "It must be awful, ending up in some old people's bungalow with no money and no friends," he said.

"Oh, Mrs Jessup isn't *poor*, exactly," said Rachel. "She's got lots of lovely things—silver-mounted photograph frames and things like that."

Terry perched on the wooden back of the seat and flicked at Rachel's curls with finger and thumb. Rachel tried to ignore him. "Old people can be quite well off," she went on to Matt. "Like I say, Mrs Jessup isn't poor—not in money. But she gets lonely." She shook her head irritably, as though she was being pestered by a fly. Terry took his hand away for a moment then continued to flick at her hair.

Matt, following Rachel's example of ignoring Terry, said, "But I thought she lived in an old people's bungalow?"

"That's what *you* said," corrected Rachel. "She lives in a bungalow but it's that pretty one with the purple clematis over the door, just past the primary school in Tavenham. And I expect she owns it—it's not Council." A harder tug at her hair made Rachel's patience snap. "Look, just leave me alone!" she shouted, jumping to her feet.

"But you got such lovely curly 'air, darling," said Terry.

"That's *my* business," snapped Rachel. "Now, push off!"

With a quick grab, Terry seized a handful of Rachel's hair and pulled her towards him. "Now it's *my* business, innit?" he leered. Rachel, forced to sit down again, gave a piercing and furious scream.

"Let her go!" said Matt angrily.

"Just watch it, sunshine," snarled Terry, pulling Rachel's head over the back of the seat by her hair. His friends watched, grinning. Then Richard said suddenly, "Look out!"

"Terry Skinner!" came a crisp voice, "go and stand outside my office in the PE corridor. At once!" It was Miss Duffy, who taught PE, striding towards them in a tracksuit with a whistle round her neck and a clipboard in her hand. She looked, Matt thought, capable of turning Terry Skinner into mincemeat.

Terry released Rachel and said, "She was bein' cheeky."

"*Get!*" said Miss Duffy with a jerk of her thumb. Terry shuffled off, flanked by his friends and grumbling loudly.

"You all right?" Miss Duffy asked Rachel.

"Yes, thank you," said Rachel, rubbing her hair. "But I'm sick of that lot—they're always mucking us about. Terry pushed Danny over this morning and you should see his knees!"

"*Right*," said Miss Duffy. She set off after Terry, looking purposeful.

Danny had stayed in the classroom during break because his knees were stiff and sore and he said it hurt to walk. The last two lessons of the day were Geography, taken by Mr Ambrose, and when everyone came in after break Danny had an exercise book open on his desk, writing busily.

"What's come over you?" asked Matt, sliding into the seat beside Danny.

"Hadn't done my Geography homework," said Danny, still writing.

"Came in handy that you hurt your knees, then," said Matt. "You'd have been chucked outside otherwise. Here—guess what happened? Terry Skinner was mucking about with Rachel, pulling her hair and being horrible, and Miss Duffy caught him at it. She marched him off to stand outside her office."

"Oh, great!" said Danny. "I hope she wallops him with a rounders bat."

"They don't hit nobody at this school," said Marcia.

"Of course they don't," said Rachel. "Mr Hazzard says it's uncivilised."

"Well, so it is," agreed Danny. "Only I don't know what they can do to people like Terry."

"There's detention," said Matt.

"Yes, but the real hard cases are in detention every night," Danny argued. "I heard Mr Potter tell someone to come for detention the other day—it was Paul Nutt in the fifth year—and Paul said, 'Can't do you a detention until Friday week, sir. I'm booked solid.' So Mr Potter gave up the idea. He doesn't want to hang about after school with people in detention, anyway. None of the teachers do."

"Mr Ambrose tried to put Marcia in detention the other day," Rachel remembered, grinning.

"I just told him I had to get the bus," said Marcia.

"But you don't go home on the bus," said Matt. "You walk, don't you?"

"Yeah," agreed Marcia. "But he don't know that. He gave me lines instead but I never done them."

"I can't imagine Terry Skinner doing lines," said Matt. "I wonder what Miss Duffy will do about him."

"If you're really awful you get suspended," said Stephen.

Rachel laughed. "Sounds like being hanged," she said.

"No, it just means you're not allowed to come to school," said Stephen.

"I know what it *means*, stupid," said Rachel. "But if they suspend Terry I should think he'll be delighted. He doesn't want to come to school anyway."

"I don't know," said Danny thoughtfully. "It's awfully boring, hanging about with nothing to do. I mean, there's not even anything to send up."

"No rules to break," agreed Matt.

Mr Potter came in with the register and Danny hastily added a few more words to what he had written. In spite of staying in during break, he still hadn't finished his homework.

CHAPTER 6

The Red Car

Matt was whistling cheerfully as he went out to the bus with the others after school. It was a bright afternoon and it looked like being a nice weekend. Not that he ever did anything very special at the weekend, but Fridays always made him feel happy.

Suddenly he stopped dead. A red car was parked on the dug-up area where the men were still interminably working on the widening of the drive. Matt looked at it, frowning. It was a Ford Escort estate. There were lots of them about, but all the same... it *could* be the same one.

Danny came hobbling up to join him. "What's the matter?" he asked.

"That car," said Matt. "It's the same sort as the one that came into the yard at Bill's farm the day I was there."

"Really?" said Danny, interested. "Are you sure? Did you get the number?"

"No, of course not," said Matt. "I didn't think there was anything suspicious about it, did I?"

Rachel and Sue arrived. "What's up?" enquired Rachel.

Matt explained, and Rachel instantly rushed across to the car, almost colliding with a man pushing a wheelbarrow. The others, grinning, saw her recoil and, although the man was out of earshot, gathered that Rachel was being subjected to some fairly colourful abuse. Arguing fiercely, she dodged round the man and went to inspect the car more closely.

The driver of the Tavenham bus started his engine and, leaning out of the window, shouted, "Are you lot coming on this bus or not?"

"Quick!" said Sue, alarmed. "He'll go without us!"

Everyone scrambled aboard and Rachel came running back, waving wildly at the driver to wait for her.

"Not a blooming taxi, you know," the driver grumbled as he set off down the cluttered drive.

Rachel tumbled into her seat beside Sue and gasped, "Piece of paper, quick, before I forget!"

"Forget what?" asked Sue, fishing in her bag.

"Car number. Thanks. Pen?"

"Oh, service with a smile," grumbled Sue, producing a felt-tip.

"W—C—F," said Rachel, writing. "Five, three, four, V. There!"

"There's no point in having the number now," said Matt. "We still don't know if it's the same car that I saw. Unless—" He looked very thoughtful. "You didn't notice anything dangling from the mirror, did you?"

"Golliwog," said Rachel promptly. "Stupid little thing, sort of knitted. Red and black."

Matt's face turned pink with excitement. "Then it *is* the same car!" he said. "And the driver was wearing a cap like farmers have, checked. And his jacket was checked, too."

"Oh, great!" said Rachel, hopping up and down on her seat with excitement. "Then *that's* the man I saw over by the cement mixer, talking to one of the workmen. Look, there he is. Quite fat. Red face."

"The workman?" asked Danny idiotically.

"No, you twit, the car driver," said Rachel. "The workman's wearing a donkey jacket."

"That's him all right," said Matt, peering out of the bus window at the two men who stood in conversation.

"But I wonder why he's talking to the road-widening man?"

"Funny," agreed Rachel. "If he's come here, it must be to see Kritz. Under cover of supplying the school with chemicals."

"More likely the road man is talking to *him*," put in Stephen. "They don't like cars being parked there."

"Oh, yes!" said Danny, remembering something. "You know when your mum picked you up from school the other day, Matt? Well, they were grumbling like anything about her parking beside the cement mixer. Going on about how they couldn't be expected to finish the job on time if people kept using the site as a car park."

"That's what the one with the wheelbarrow said," agreed Rachel. "Kids all over the place, cars parked on the site, men off sick, bad weather—he was really fed up."

"So the man in the donkey jacket was telling Mr Chemicals to move his car," said Danny.

"'Spect so," said Rachel.

"Parsons," said Matt. They all looked at him. "The man's name," he explained. "I just remembered. He got out of the car at Bill's and said he was Mr Parsons from Silcox and Waggitt."

"Oh, *good*, Matt!" said Rachel. "That's terrific!"

"But what are we going to *do*?" asked Sue impatiently. "We've got the missing link now, haven't we? Plum and Creepy knew where the school video stuff was kept and so it was pinched. Mr Parsons knew where Mr North's stuff was kept and he told Kritz and Plum."

"And it gets pinched," Rachel agreed. "Or almost, anyway."

They all looked at each other. Then Matt said, "Well, there's only one thing we can do. We'll have to tell the police."

"Yes," said Rachel with a gusty sigh. "Then they'll have all the fun. Shame, really."

"We can't actually arrest people, though," Danny pointed out. "That's what the police are for."

"Oh, I know that," agreed Rachel regretfully. Then she brightened. "Still, there's nothing to stop us keeping an eye open, is there? Whether the police know or not?"

"Nothing at all," agreed Matt. "Pity it's a Saturday tomorrow—we could have gone into Flaxton after school if it had been a week day."

"There's a police house in Tavenham," Rachel reminded him.

Matt frowned. "Is there? Where?"

"Down past the telephone exchange," said Danny. "Red-brick house with cabbages in the garden. There's usually a panda car outside."

"Oh, yes, of course!" said Matt. "But it isn't an actual police *station*, is it?"

"'Course it is," said Rachel.

"We went there when Higgins got lost," said Sue. "He was ever so nice. Someone had found him and handed him in and he had him in the back of his car."

"Who had who?" asked Danny, confused.

"Mr Birkett, the policeman," Sue said patiently, "had Higgins, our Jack Russell. In the back of—"

"Well, anyway," said Matt, "we're going to this police house now, are we? As soon as the bus gets to Tavenham?"

"Yes," said Rachel.

"I'm not," said Danny. "I really don't fancy long walks. And I've got to do that Geography homework again. He marked it in class and slung it back. Said it was rubbish."

"Poor Danny," said Sue, "I bet your knees hurt."

"They sort of ache," said Danny.

"I still wish it was Monday tomorrow," said Matt. "With all this going on, it seems awful, having to do nothing for two whole days." And only a short time ago he had been looking forward to the weekend.

"Never mind," Rachel consoled him. "Tomorrow you're coming to see Mrs Jessup with me, remember? That'll pass some time away."

Matt groaned inwardly. But having just said that he had nothing to do, there was no getting out of it. "All right," he said, "I'll come."

P.C. Burkett was having his tea. His wife opened the door into the kitchen and said, "Geoff, there's three kiddies here with something to tell you about the break-in at Mill Green."

"Are there, now?" said Mr Burkett, pushing his plate away and brushing crumbs off his blue shirt. His tunic hung on the chair behind him. "Come on in, you three, and tell me all about it. Any more tea in the pot, love?" he asked his wife.

"I'll make some fresh," she said. "You kiddies all take milk and sugar, do you?"

Matt and Sue nodded and Rachel said, "No sugar for me." They glanced at each other, amused and slightly irritated at being called "kiddies".

P.C. Burkett reached behind him for his tunic and fished in a pocket for his notebook. "Right," he said. "Now, what's it all about?"

Rachel plunged into an account of their suspicions but, even to Matt, it sounded terribly jumbled.

"Now, hang on," said Mr Burkett, holding up a hand. "Let's start at the beginning, shall we? You're telling me you know who took this stuff, are you?"

"We know who *might* have taken it," corrected Matt.

"Ah," said P.C. Burkett. "Now, that's a very different thing, isn't it? Oh, thank you, love."

His wife filled his cup then poured tea for Matt, Rachel and Sue. She took the lid off a tin of biscuits and offered it round, then left it on the table as they all munched gratefully. "Kiddies are always hungry," she said comfortably. "Just help yourselves."

Despite the biscuits, Matt found it an embarrassing interview. P.C. Burkett was patient and kind, but Matt had the feeling that he considered their suspicions rather silly. "We get quite a lot of this sort of thing whenever there's an incident concerning a school," he said, half to his wife and half to Matt, whom he seemed to regard as the most sensible of the three. "There's always an unpopular teacher—with good reason, perhaps; I'm not saying all teachers are what they ought to be. And when something like this happens it's a great temptation to put two and two together and make about six and a half!" He smiled at their crestfallen faces and added, "But I'm very pleased you came to see me. Any help from the public is welcome, and we'll certainly take a note of what you've told me. Let's get your names down, to start with, and where you live."

It all took a remarkably long time. P.C. Burkett was meticulously careful about checking the spelling of each name and insisted on having the exact time and place of everything the children had seen. He wrote down the number of the red Escort, a description of Mr Parsons, of Kritz and of Miss Plumforth, together with details of what they did and of their various connections with Mill Green School. Then he wrote down the facts about the injury to Kritz's hand and his well-timed visit to the hospital. "We can easily check that, of course," he said.

At last it was all done. Sue had stifled a yawn once or twice, and even Rachel was beginning to look a bit bored. Matt thought that, compared with the thrillers he had read, being a policeman in real life wasn't very dangerous. In fact, it seemed rather a nice job. As if reading his mind, P.C. Burkett smiled suddenly and said, "Not very exciting, is it? I'm afraid we don't go round having flashes of inspiration like they do in books. Police work for the most part depends on being very thorough. Making sure you don't miss anything."

When Matt, Rachel and Sue got up to go, Mrs Burkett said, "Well, I think it's nice to see some youngsters who have got the sense to come and tell you when they think something's wrong. Most kiddies these days wouldn't take the trouble."

"Yes, indeed," agreed her husband. Then he added, "I don't want you three to start playing the detective, though. If anything else happens, come and tell me by all means, but don't try to do anything about it yourselves. Crime isn't a game. There's quite a lot of risk involved and it's best left to the professionals. So don't go doing anything silly. Right?"

They all nodded, though Matt heard Rachel mutter under her breath, "Spoil-sport!"

"Days are drawing in," said Mrs Burkett as she ushered them out into the fading daylight. They waved as they went down the path between the cabbages and she waved back, then shut the door.

"It must be awfully late," said Matt, breaking into a trot. "Mum will be wondering where on earth I am."

"See you tomorrow, then," said Rachel. "I'll come and pick you up in the afternoon. I go to drama class in the morning."

Matt turned, hopping backwards because he was still in a hurry. "What time?" he asked.

"Three-ish. She's really nice, Matt, honest."

"She'd better be," said Matt over his shoulder, and set off for home.

Rather to his surprise, Matt had to admit that Mrs Jessup *was* rather nice. She was very small and slender, with a shock of white curly hair and dark eyes which gave a lively look to her thin face. When she opened the door to Matt and Rachel she was wearing a gathered skirt and several sweaters on top of each other. Her feet were encased in furry boots topped by collapsing scarlet leg-warmers over purple tights. Evidently she felt the cold. She clasped her hands theatrically and said, "Darlings! How lovely to see you! Come along in at once and sit by the fire. I'll make some tea. Do you like crumpets? I bought *heaps* of crumpets this morning because they looked so nice and then thought, you silly old thing, how on earth are you going to eat all that lot? So I'm terribly glad you came."

She led the way into the sitting room where firelight glinted on what seemed to Matt a multitude of faces. Framed photographs crowded every surface and lined the walls, each one signed across the corner with a flamboyant scrawl—"To darling Dodie with all my love. Bebe." "Wonderful days at the Folies. Max." Many of the pictures featured a curly-haired, dark-eyed girl in a variety of amazing costumes, standing in a dancing pose or being hugged by beaming people who were, Matt assumed, celebrities. With a slight shock, he realised that the girl was Mrs Jessup.

"This is Matt," said Rachel. "He's come to be helpful."

"How kind of you, Matt," said Mrs Jessup. "How do you do?" She extended a formal hand. "Dodie Jessup. Dodie Lamont, as was. But that would be before your time."

"Matt Aiken," Matt responded politely, shaking hands. Mrs Jessup's fingers, he noticed, were knobbly and bent. Seeing his glance, Mrs Jessup stroked the misshapen knuckles ruefully and said, "Stupid arthritis. That's why I can't manage a screwdriver very well these days. So humiliating, isn't it, to lose control of a simple thing like a screwdriver."

"Rachel said you've got a shelf that wants fixing," said Matt.

"If you can fix that, you'll be my friend for life," said Mrs Jessup. "But we'll have our crumpets first. The shelf isn't hungry and we are."

"I want to hear more about when you were on the stage," said Rachel. "Oh, and they say at school you've got to sign a form to say you don't mind."

"How curious," said Mrs Jessup. "I have been interviewed on many occasions but nobody ever asked me to sign a form."

Rachel dug in her anorak pocket and produced a tattered notebook, folded and grubby, out of which she produced the equally dog-eared form. Then she dug again for a pencil. "If only my spelling was better," she said mournfully. "I don't think Mr Potter takes me seriously. And I *do* want to be chosen to do a filmed interview. You never know, it might be my big chance."

Mrs Jessup laughed. "Schools aren't in the big chance business," she said. "Leave it all behind you, my dear, and start to live in the real world, then you get your chances." She went across to the kitchen which opened off the far side of the living room, and Matt saw that she walked a little stiffly. He suspected that the "stupid arthritis" had affected more than her fingers.

"It's all very well," said Rachel, "but I've got *years* of school before I can leave, and I might as well make the best of it."

"Why don't you use a tape recorder?" asked Mrs Jessup from the kitchen.

Rachel hit herself on the forehead with a clenched fist. "Why didn't I think of that?" she asked. "Brilliant!"

"I expect the school would have lent you one," said Matt, "if they hadn't been pinched. Were they *all* stolen, do you know?"

"No idea," said Rachel. "But I can't imagine they'd lend me one, not with all this panic about burglars going on."

"You can use mine," said Mrs Jessup, appearing at the kitchen door in an apron with a large picture of a sauce bottle on it. "My daughter bought it for me before she went to America. She sends me tapes instead of letters. Like you, she is not very good at spelling. It's quite a nice tape recorder, I think. Made in Japan. When I was young they only made fans and paper flowers. Oh, the crumpets!" She disappeared again, calling back, "Shall we have tea by the fire?"

"Oh, lovely," said Rachel. She went across to the kitchen. "Did I tell you, Mrs Jessup, we think we know who took the stuff from school? We went to the police yesterday. Don't they write *slowly?* I suppose they've got to make sure there aren't any mistakes. It's ever so boring, though."

Matt went and stood at the kitchen door.

"Oh, terribly boring," agreed Mrs Jessup, buttering the first lot of crumpets. "A friend of mine had her costume stolen—Military Maisie, she called herself. She was a stipper. And it wasn't the first time, poor dear, so the management called the police."

"I thought strippers didn't wear any clothes," said Rachel, puzzled.

"They don't when they've taken them off," said Mrs

Jessup. "But you can't take them off if you haven't got them on, can you? But it was wonderful hearing this policeman writing down every item so seriously. 'Ostrich feathers, three. Spangles, gold, two. Spurs, two. Er—lower half of bathing costume, one.'"

"I still wish we could catch the thieves ourselves," said Rachel. "P.C. Burkett said we weren't to get involved but it must be terrific fun if you could actually catch them red-handed."

Matt thought about Bill's grim amusement when Rachel had used that phrase once before. He thought, too, of the phrase the policeman had used, "Crime isn't a game." He wondered how much damage a dog's teeth would really do, and how long it would take for the injuries to heal. Kritz had replaced the bandage on his hand with the black fingerstall the very next day. So could he have been very badly bitten? He was the kind who would make a terrific fuss about anything. If he really had been a doctor in his own country, as he said, then perhaps he welcomed any injury with maximum bandages.

"Wake up, Matt," said Rachel, pushing a lace-edged tablecloth at him. "Mrs Jessup says we'll use the round table by the fire—but you'll have to take the photographs off it."

By the time Rachel and Matt started out on their bikes for home, it was getting dark.

"Wasn't it super of Mrs Jessup to say I could borrow her tape recorder!" said Rachel. "Now I can do a really *good* interview—just you wait! Pity her son's coming to see her tomorrow or I could have done it then. I'm sure we've got a blank cassette at home."

"Couldn't you have used your own tape recorder?" asked Matt.

"It's too big," said Rachel. "Part of Dad's stereo system. Not the sort of thing you can carry about. No, hers'll be great. She's super, isn't she? *My* granny rambles on about wind-up gramophones."

"When are you going to do your interview, then?" asked Matt.

"Monday after school," said Rachel.

Matt nodded. "I'll come with you," he said. "I've chopped plenty of firewood but I felt a twit, not being able to fix that shelf. The rawlplug's come out of the wall, you see, and the screw won't hold and she hasn't got any replacement ones. We've got some rawlplugs at home, so I'll bring some on Monday. If the hole's a bit big you can hammer a couple of broken-off match sticks in beside the plug. It always holds then."

"Aren't you clever!" said Rachel admiringly. "My dad does all that sort of thing."

"Yes," said Matt. "I expect he does." Rachel bit her lip, and Matt knew she had just remembered that his father didn't live with them. But he thought with sudden pleasure of the rack of tools he and his mother had collected together since they had been living in Tavenham.

"My dad goes mad if anyone touches his tools," Rachel went on. "We're not even allowed in the garage."

Matt smiled. "Tough luck," he said.

CHAPTER 7

Crime Isn't a Game

"I must say," remarked Mr Hazzard, "I feel a little hurt." He stared at Matt, Rachel and Sue reproachfully. "Surely," he went on, "if you had any light to throw on a situation which concerns the school so seriously, you should have come to see me about it."

They nodded guiltily.

"It's a bit shattering," the Headmaster went on, "to arrive at school on a Monday morning to find a police car on the premises once again, and this time with some James Bond-type story dreamed up by the three of our own people. I can appreciate that you meant well, and of course I'm happy to know that you're on the side of law and order, as all right-minded people should be. But how do you think I felt to have the police telling me this far-fetched story about two members of my own staff?"

Matt shuffled uneasily. He had not expected P.C. Burkett to get in touch with Mr Hazzard. He felt vaguely let down.

Mr Hazzard had not finished. "Mr Kritz," he said, "has suffered from political persecution in a way which we in Britain find it difficult to imagine. It makes me very sad to think that he should meet an atmosphere of suspicion here at this school. I think you must be very lacking in imagination if you can't see what you are doing. Or perhaps it is too much imgination you're suffering from. Miss Plumforth — a student who has hardly been with us for more than a couple of days? What can you be thinking of?"

"But—" began Sue, then bit her lip and was silent. Her round face was puckered with worry.

"Well?" asked Mr Hazzard.

"She means, it all seemed to fit," said Rachel, coming to Sue's rescue. "It looked as if it *had* to be them. We didn't mean to do anything to hurt Mr Kritz, honestly," she went on, "or Miss Plumforth. We didn't think they'd even know—not if they hadn't done it, that is."

Mr Hazzard sighed. "Rachel," he said, "that's very naive, isn't it? When you go to the police, you are setting off a process which won't stop until it has done its job to the best of its ability. Rather like starting up a machine. It's not the same as talking to each other or even to a teacher. I expect the policeman you saw wrote down everything you told him, didn't he?"

They all nodded.

"There you are, you see," said Mr Hazzard. "You have made an official complaint against two people who are most probably entirely innocent, haven't you?"

Matt thought about it. Then he said bravely, "But what if they aren't, sir?" Mr Hazzard looked at him and Matt met his gaze squarely. There was a silence. Then Mr Hazzard conceded, "We have to face that possibility if it comes. All I'm saying, Matt, is that another time, I'd rather know before you tell anyone else. All right?"

"Yes," said Matt.

Rachel looked as if she was going to burst into tears. "I'm awfully sorry," she said. "I never thought of it like that. Upsetting you and everything."

Mr Hazzard smiled kindly. "I know you didn't," he said, "but we all learn by experience. Now, you'd better get along to your form room or we'll be late for Assembly. I'll be having a word with Mr Potter about all this later on today."

With murmurs of, "Yes, sir," they went quietly out and shut the door.

"He makes you feel so *awful,*" said Rachel.

"Like Matt said, though," Sue pointed out, "we still don't *know* Creepy and Plum didn't do it."

"I don't think Kritz was at the farm," said Matt, trying to be fair. "His hand isn't bad enough for a dog to have savaged it. But he still could be the spy."

They set off towards the form room, thinking hard.

"Matt's right," said Rachel to Sue. "I can see how Mr Hazzard feels, but it doesn't actually change anything. The man in the red car was at the farm and he was here. There's got to be a connection. And Kritz could well be it."

"I just wish we could prove it," said Matt. "One way or the other."

"I bet we can," said Rachel, with a return of her usual optimism. "All we need is a lucky break."

The bell pealed for Assembly and a general rumble began as people got to their feet in every classroom in the school, pushing chairs under desks and grabbing the opportunity for a quick burst of conversation. Doors were opened and the noise swelled, punctuated by teachers shouting for quiet.

"Come on," said Rachel. "Quick, before they all come out."

In another moment the corridors would be jammed with people surging towards the hall. Rachel took to her heels and pelted off towards the form room, the other two close behind her.

Mr Hazzard wore his gown for Assembly, and Matt, sitting on the floor with the others, thought the Headmaster seemed like a different person. He spoke more loudly and slowly, and did not look anybody in the eye although he gave the impression that he saw everything that was going on.

"You will be glad to hear," he was saying, "the contractors assure me that the work on widening the drive will be completed this week. Some of your parents have complained about reduced parking facilities while this work has been going on, and there seem to have been a few unfortunate clashes of personality about this question of parking cars. So will you all please tell your parents that the end is in sight, and ask them to be as patient as possible for these last few days. We do regret the inconvenience but of course the work will result in much improved access to the school."

"Still can't see why they didn't get it right in the first place," muttered Danny, who was sitting with his legs, resplendent in brand-new trousers, stuck straight out in front of him because they were still too stiff and bruised to bend.

Mr Hazzard's gaze rested in Danny's direction for a moment, then he went on, "Turning to another and even less pleasant topic, it was brought to my notice on Friday that some members of senior forms have been bullying younger children. This is a particularly disgusting thing to do and I will *not* tolerate it. In a civilised community the large should look after the small, the strong protect the weak. One person has already been suspended from school, and I would ask you all to be on your guard about this. If you see it going on, don't turn a blind eye. The victims of bullying are in need of your help, whoever you are, just as the victim in our reading this morning about the Good Samaritan was in need of help. Now, we will sing hymn number seven hundred and one, 'Ye Holy Angels Bright'."

Mrs Gipsum struck up the tune on the piano and the school straggled half-heartedly into song. Despite all that practice, Matt thought, it didn't sound much better. As he went through the motions of singing he thought about the day that lay ahead. "Assist our song", the school carolled raggedly. "For else the theme too high doth seem—" The first two lessons were Science. With Miss Plumforth. "M'm," said Matt to himself thoughtfully.

Unfortunately the verse had just ended and the sound which Matt made landed exactly in the moment of silence before Mrs Gipsum struck the opening chord again. Matt blushed violently as everyone round him giggled and Mrs Gipsum glared down from the piano on the stage. Matt tried to look apologetic but, judging from the increased volume of Mrs Gipsum's playing and the way she continued to glower in his direction, he hadn't succeeded.

Miss Plumforth came into the lab looking pink and determined. Kritz, who had stayed in his room with the door shut while the form made its noisy entry, now came and stood by the demonstration bench as if lending moral support.

"You can see he's a kind of henchman," Debbie whispered. "He looks as if he's going to *murder* anyone who misbehaves."

Kritz did, indeed, look grim. He stood with his hands thrust into the pockets of his white overall and stared at the class with tight-lipped dislike.

"How's your hand—sir?" asked Michael Chalmers.

There was a general giggle at the irony in Michael's voice, but Kritz looked pleased. "Much better," he said with a slight bow. "Thank you." Everyone giggled again.

"Today we are going to do a different kind of testing," announced Miss Plumforth.

"Burning all them things out of the oil?" asked John hopefully.

"No," said Miss Plumforth. "Mr Dodds says he would prefer to do that with you himself at a later date."

"Don't blame him," said Bill North audibly.

"Today," Miss Plumforth continued, "we are going to test acidity and alkalinity. Now, does anyone know what is meant by these words?"

Nobody said anything. Matt glanced round the room and saw that they were all looking at Miss Plumforth with a bright but totally unco-operative interest. "Oh, come on," she said with an uneasy laugh. "I'm sure you can think of something that's acid, at least."

"Acid drops," said John Beasley helpfully, but nobody laughed. He pulled a packet of sweets out of his pocket and pointed triumphantly to the lettering on the side. "See? 'Acid-drops'. S'right, innit?"

Miss Plumforth smiled encouragingly. "Some forms of acid are widely used for flavouring, yes," she said. "Citric acid in particular. Anything else?"

The silence was almost oppressive. Matt, who could think of several answers, did not put up his hand but glanced at Rachel. She raised her eyebrows and gave a faint shrug. If the class had decided in some tacit way to be mulish, then she would go along with it. And so would Matt.

"Come along," said Miss Plumforth again. "I expect you've been in a bit of a row for being so noisy last week and the week before, but that doesn't mean you can't find your voices to answer a question. Now, just think of something that's acid."

"Lemons is," said Marcia, bored. She looked up from filing her nails and said, "You better just get on with it, Miss."

"I do wish you would put that nail file away," said

Miss Plumforth irritably. She looked flustered. Suddenly John said from the back of the class, "'Ere, Miss—"

"Yes?" said Miss Plumforth hopefully.

"Are you a friend of that bloke that drives the red car?" John asked baldly. "The one who brings the chemicals and things?"

Miss Plumforth looked blank. "No, I'm afraid not," she said. "Mr Dodds deals with all that sort of thing—it's nothing to do with me."

There was a buzz of conversation.

"Well, then—do you know anyone who's been bitten by a dog lately?" demanded John.

Several people said, "Shut *up*, John," and there was a lot of giggling.

Rachel turned to Matt and said, "How did *he* know about it?"

"Oh, everybody knows," said Matt. "Only John's so tactless."

Now that the silence had been broken, a rising tide of noise had taken its place. Miss Plumforth said, "Do be quiet," several times but nobody even heard her. She leaned her hands on the bench and stared down at them, and the plaits of fair hair coiled round her head made her look very young. Suddenly Matt felt sorry for her.

Kritz stepped forward. "Right," he said incisively. "Now you all listening, please."

Everyone looked at him, surprised. He waited until they were silent, then he said, "You all laughing at my English. Very funny—big joke. Okay." He shrugged. "I am speaking lousy English. I am speaking lousy Hungarian, too, and Serbo-Croat and Russian and German. How many languages you are speaking? Little bit French, maybe? Is taking a long time to be speaking it very good, you are finding? So I am finding, too." He made a dismissive gesture and everyone noticed that the black fingerstall had been replaced by a small Band-aid.

"But this not the question," Kritz went on. "Question is, this lesson. Look." He fished in his pocket and held up a small strip of mauve paper. "This is called litmus paper. Very useful stuff. Turning blue for alkalines, red for acids. You having solution—" he held up an imaginary beaker—"you not knowing what it is. Testing with litmus paper." He dipped the strip of paper into the invisible beaker. "Telling you acid or alkaline. Is a *tool*, you see?" he demanded emphatically, impatient with their failure to see this simple fact. "Like, you wanting to know how big something is, you measuring. You want to know how air in tyre?" He bent down and applied an imaginary pressure gauge and said, "Pff!" Everyone nodded. "How hot something?" he went on. "Using thermometer. Shelf on wall straight?" He levelled an invisible tool between his hands, squinting at it critically, and several people said, "Spirit level!" He nodded enthusiastically and gave a sudden smile. "Is *tool*, you see!" he repeated.

"Oh!" said Peter Box as light dawned. "Well, why didn't she *say*?"

"She was trying to," said Marcia, inspecting her nails. She fished in her large orange bag and got out a bottle of red varnish.

"You putting that away!" cried Kritz in outrage. "At once!"

Marcia grinned. "Okay, chief," she said.

Everyone laughed, including Miss Plumforth.

"Go on, then, Miss," said Felicity encouragingly. "Tell us about this mauve stuff."

Kritz stepped back with a gesture to Miss Plumforth as if to tell her that the stage was hers. She smiled at him. As Miss Plumforth began to speak, Rachel looked at Matt with a hopeless sigh and a shrug. He knew what she meant. Kritz and Plum suddenly didn't seem creepy any more. It was a pity, for they had been ideal people to suspect of being criminals. It seemed now that the hunt for the Mill Green spy was right back at square one.

The rest of the day was boringly uneventful, and Matt was glad he and Rachel were going to see Mrs Jessup after school. Secretly, he was quite looking forward to it.

Terry Skinner was lounging against a gatepost outside the school as the buses started to move out.

"What's he doing here?" said Stephen Chuff, looking out of the window. "I though he'd been suspended."

"He has," said Sue. "Debbie's brother is in the same form as him, and *he* said he has."

"I expect he's come to see his friends," said Matt.

Danny said, "Told you it was boring, being suspended, didn't I? You remember Kevin Evans and that lot? Well, they were suspended for ages because of that business about the fire, and they kept coming back to school. Mr Watts kept chucking them out, but the next morning there they were again."

"Must want their heads read," said Stephen. "If anyone told me to stay away from school I'd be delighted."

"Chuffed?" suggested Rachel.

"Oh, ha, ha," said Stephen witheringly.

"I hope Terry tries to come back," said Matt. "Mr Watts might be so busy throwing him out that he won't have time to take us for Maths."

"Some hopes," said Rachel.

When the bus arrived at Tavenham, Matt went home to collect his bicycle before going off with Rachel to see Mrs Jessup. His mother, who got home early from her job at the library on Mondays, had tea ready when he arrived and would not hear of him going out again without having something to eat first. Rachel rang the door bell while Matt was still finishing his beans on toast and was easily persuaded to come in for a cup of tea and a bit of chocolate cake. As a result, it was getting dark by the time they set out for Mrs Jessup's house.

"She'll think we're not coming," said Rachel, pedalling hard.

"I know," said Matt. "I'm awfully sorry. Mum seems to think school meals are all crisps and Coke now they don't do the meat and veg system." He fell back to let a lorry overtake them then caught up again and added, "She's convinced I'm half starved."

"Lovely," said Rachel. "Mine's on a muesli and brown rice kick at the moment. Boring."

It was not far to Mrs Jessup's bungalow and they saw the light in her sitting room shining pinkly through the flowered curtains as they came up the dark lane. They turned in at Mrs Jessup's front gate, which stood open, walked their bikes up the garden path and leaned them carefully against the wall of the bungalow. Adding to the glow from behind the curtains was the flickering bluish light of a television set.

Rachel fished in her saddlebag for the blank cassette. "Did you remember those things for the shelf?" she asked Matt.

"Rawlplugs. Yes, I've got them in my pocket," said Matt. "And some new screws."

"Good," said Rachel.

They went to the front door and rang the bell.

"I hope she's not getting tea for us," said Matt, struck by a sudden thought. "I don't think I could eat *another* tea."

"I could," said Rachel happily. "I think Mum's doing

cheese and lentil pie. Yukky." She listened. There was no sound of Mrs Jessup coming to the door.

"She might not hear the bell if she's in the kitchen." said Matt, putting his finger on the push again. At the same time, Rachel banged on the knocker. They looked at each other and giggled rather guiltily. "Wake the dead," said Rachel.

There was a long pause. Matt frowned. "She *must* have heard that," he said.

"Must have done," agreed Rachel. "She's not in the least bit deaf."

"She's got the television on, though," said Matt. "You can see it through the curtains."

"But it isn't loud, or we could hear it." Rachel was beginning to look worried. "Matt, I think there's something wrong. What if she's been taken ill? What if she's lying on the kitchen floor with a broken leg and can't call for help or—"

"Now, hang on," said Matt. "Don't start panicking. If you think something like that has happened we'd better go round the back and have a look."

"Oh, Matt," said Rachel gratefully, "you are *sensible*. I knew you were the right person to bring. I thought of Stephen at first, because he's good at hammers and things, but he's always so busy on that smallholding, I didn't think he'd want to bother. And things are a bit funny about his brother at the moment. But you're *lovely*."

"Oh, shut up," said Matt, embarrassed.

They were following the path round the side of the house. Light streamed across the lawn from the uncurtained kitchen window. Rachel ran ahead of Matt and looked in. Then she gave an odd, strangled yelp.

"What's the matter?" asked Matt. Rachel had ducked away from the window and was crouching in the shadow of the wall below it. She flapped at him frantically to keep down and, feeling silly, he crept towards her in a doubled-up position. "What's the *matter*?" he demanded again in a rather cross whisper. Rachel's flair for the dramatic could go a bit far sometimes.

"There's a man," Rachel breathed. "In there. Oh, Matt!"

She was close to tears.

Very cautiously, Matt straightened up and peeped through the edge of the window. And then he understood why Rachel was upset.

Mrs Jessup was sitting on a wooden chair with her feet sticking out sideways as if she had just been pushed into it. She had both hands over her face. A man stood in front of her in an attitude of menace, a hand upraised. He looked very big, a threatening, angular shape in a navy blue donkey jacket.

Matt watched in frozen horror. Slowly, the man relaxed his threatening attitude, and Matt realised that he had been listening for another ring at the front door bell.

"They've gone away," said the man. "Right. Up." He grabbed Mrs Jessup's arm and yanked her to her feet with as little effort as if she had been a rag doll. "Money," said the man. "And quick. I got most of what I want but there's more than this, got to be. Where's your bag?"

"You're being very silly," Matt heard Mrs Jessup begin to say. The man slapped her across the side of the head. Matt felt the pain like a shock wave between his own ears and for an awful moment he thought he was going to be sick. Unbidden, P.C. Burkett's words came back to him. "Crime isn't a game." Too right.

"Matt," whispered Rachel frantically. "What are we going to do?"

Matt did not dare to let himself stop and think. "We've got to go in," he said.

CHAPTER 8

The Intruder

Rachel nodded. Her face was very white.

Matt didn't wait to say anything else. He turned the knob of the back door and walked in. The man, who was pushing Mrs Jessup ahead of him into the sitting room, jumped round. He held one arm across his chest in an awkward sort of way, Matt saw, and his dark-stubbled face was contorted with consternation at the sight of the unexpected visitors. For a long second nobody moved and it flashed through Matt's mind that if the man attacked them there was nothing much he and Rachel could do about it.

Then Mrs Jessup began to scream. With both hands to her face she screamed in a high-pitched, demented way, like a mad thing, over and over again. It was a horrifying sound. The man pushed her violently away from him and she tottered backwards, colliding with the round table where she and Matt and Rachel had eaten buttered crumpets only two days ago. Scattering framed photographs, she crashed to the floor. As if frantically seeking shelter, she tried to crawl towards the sofa, then collapsed and lay whimpering on the carpet. Matt felt frozen. Things seemed to be happening with a paralysed slowness. The man stepped carefully backwards, his eyes fixed on Matt and Rachel like someone confronted by a tiger. He groped behind him for the handle of the door to the hall, opened it and bolted out of the house through the front door. Matt shot after him.

The man ran in an oddly lurching, lopsided way down the front path, jumped in a car parked by the hedge and started it up. Matt reached the open gate as the car's lights were switched on and its engine screamed into life. With a spurt of gravel from under the tyres and a wild slewing from side to side, the car roared off down the lane. But Matt had seen the number illuminated in a surrounding patch of red paintwork. WCF 534V.

Matt rushed back into the house. His heart was pounding in his chest. "He's gone off in the red Escort!" he said. "*The* red Escort—I saw the number!"

Rachel did not answer. She was kneeling on the floor beside Mrs Jessup, saying, "It's all right. It's all right. The man's gone." Slowly, Mrs Jessup struggled to a sitting position. Then she began to cry. Matt, seeing the old lady's face for the first time, felt a renewed sense of shock. Under the mop of curly white hair, the features which had been so neat and composed were bruised and swollen. One eye was almost closed and a cut lip spilled a dribble of blood down her chin. Rachel put her arms round Mrs Jessup as if the old lady was a child. "Oh, there," she said, uselessly. "There." Tears were welling up in her own eyes.

Matt said, "Where's the telephone? I've got to get the police." He still felt terribly sick but he tried to ignore it.

"In the hall," said Rachel, ducking her head to rub her eyes on her sleeve. Mrs Jessup made a groping movement with one hand towards the sofa, and Rachel added quickly, "Come and help, Matt."

Together they half lifted and half pulled the old lady on to the sofa. Although she tried to help them there seemed to be no strength in her limbs and she had started to shiver violently.

Matt went into the hall where the telephone stood with a vase of chrysanthemums beside it on a polished oval table. He looked at the telephone directory and thought, Burkett. He was dismayed at the prospect of having to look up the policeman's number. He didn't want to cope with anything as complicated as that. He just wanted help. Quickly.

"Nine-nine-nine!" shouted Rachel from the sitting room as if reading Matt's thoughts. He dialled, mentally kicking himself for not thinking of something so obvious straight away.

"Which service?" a voice asked almost immediately.

"Police," said Matt.

Rachel ran past him to the bedroom. "Must find a blanket," she said. "She seems so cold."

"Police," said a man's voice.

"An old lady's been attacked," said Matt. "Mrs Jessup. We came to see her and this man was here." His voice sounded jumpy and he wasn't explaining very well but he struggled on. "He'd been hitting her. She's all bruised and—"

"What address?" asked the voice calmly.

"I don't know what the house is called," said Matt, kicking himself again. "It's a bungalow, just past the primary school."

"What village?"

"Oh—Tavenham." Matt felt as if his insides were churning about and he didn't seem able to think straight. Rachel came past him again with her arms full of a bundled-up duvet.

"And your name?" enquired the voice.

"Matt Aiken. Er—Matthew," Matt corrected himself, supposing that the police didn't deal in nicknames. And why were they bothering with things like that, anyway? "You will come, won't you?" he asked anxiously.

"Be with you as soon as we can," said the voice with its impeccable calm, and the line purred in Matt's ear. He replaced the receiver and went into the sitting room.

Mrs Jessup, huddled in the duvet, looked very small. Her face was even more puffy now, and the bruises were darkening, but she tried to smile at Matt when he came in. Rachel was sitting on the arm of the sofa beside her, looking worried. She touched the old lady's hand and asked, "Mrs Jessup, would you like a cup of tea?"

"Yes," whispered Mrs Jessup, who was still shivering. "Please."

Rachel went into the kitchen, and Matt heard her filling the kettle. She came to the doorway and asked, "What were you saying about a car, Matt? It was the red Escort?"

"Yes," said Matt. "Parked in the hedge, just down the road. It was the same number. I saw it." Mrs Jessup was watching them fearfully, as if she was still afraid that her attacker might return.

"But it wasn't the chemicals man," said Rachel.

"Parsons. No, it wasn't," Matt agreed. "But I've seen him before. I'm sure I have." He was beginning to feel a little better. Life was settling down again, with kettles boiling and people talking. The dream-like experience of finding the man in the house was over. Rachel found the tea in a tin with a picture of bluetits on it and looked round for the teapot.

"It should be here, on the shelf," she said. "It's a silver one. I remember from when I helped her wash up on Saturday."

There was a sound from the sitting room as if Mrs Jessup was trying to say something. Matt went to see.

"Had a bag." Despite the duvet, the old lady was still shivering. "Taking all my things. Teapot."

"He didn't have a bag when he went out," said Matt.

"So it must be here." His sick horror was beginning to be replaced by anger at the man who had done this to little Mrs Jessup. He clenched his fists as he went back to the kitchen. If he could get his hands on that man . . . but Matt knew he was deluding himself. The man had been here, and there had been no question of Matt getting his hands on him. The reality had been far too frightening.

Rachel had found the black zipper bag on the pantry floor and was at the sink, swishing some hot water in the teapot. "It's so horrible to think of his beastly hands all over her things," she said. "The photographs in that bag—they're of people she's loved, but he just wanted them for the silver frames." She put three teabags in the pot and added, "I thought catching criminals would be exciting, but I just feel sort of—dirty."

Matt nodded. He knew exactly what she meant. At that moment there was a loud knock at the front door.

Mrs Jessup gave a little cry of alarm and shrank inside her duvet. "It's all right," Matt assured her as he went to the door. "It'll be the police."

It was a young policeman and a policewoman who stood on the doorstep. "An old lady been attacked?" said the policeman.

"Yes," said Matt, standing back to let them in. "It was me who rang up."

As they came into the sitting room Rachel came through the kitchen door with a tray of tea, and Matt saw that the round table was still almost in the lap of the armchair by the fire, where Mrs Jessup's fall had sent it skidding across the floor. The policeman set it more centrally and smiled at Rachel as she lowered her tray on to it.

"That's a good girl," said the policewoman approvingly. She bent over Mrs Jessup and said,

"You're all right, my love, we're here to take care of you. Can you sit up and have a cup of tea, or does anything hurt a lot?"

"I'm all right," said Mrs Jessup. Her usually clear voice was blurred by her swollen lips but she looked a little stronger.

"I'll get two more cups," said Rachel.

"Now," said the policeman, taking off his cap to reveal bushy red hair, "when did all this happen?"

Matt and Rachel explained step by step exactly what they had seen, while the policeman wrote it all down on sheets of lined paper with printing along the top, and the policewoman sat on the sofa beside Mrs Jessup, watching her carefully as the old lady drank her cup of tea.

"Had you seen this man before?" asked the policeman.

"No," said Rachel. "Don't think so."

The policeman looked enquiringly at Matt, who was frowning. "I think I have," he said. "But I can't think where."

"About six feet two," the policeman read back from what he had written. "Forty-ish, no beard or moustache but badly shaved. Dark hair, wearing navy blue donkey jacket and jeans."

"Bandage," said Mrs Jessup suddenly. Everyone looked at her. "Bandage on his arm," she said. "Sticking out from his sleeve. Very dirty bandage."

Matt and Rachel looked at each other with sudden excitement. "Mr North's dog!" said Rachel. "Bill said there was a bit of dark material in its mouth and that donkey jacket *was* a bit ragged!"

"Ah!" said the policeman. "You're talking about the attempted break-in at the farm last week?"

"Yes—and it's the same car, you see," said Matt,

"like I told you. It belongs to Mr Parsons, of Silcox and Waggitt, because I saw it at North's farm. But it wasn't Mr Parsons driving it tonight."

"The plot *does* thicken, doesn't it?" said the policeman with interest, writing again. "We can check that number, of course, and we'll have a little talk with Mr Parsons. And you think you've seen this man before?"

Matt racked his brains. Was he just imagining that the man's face was familiar? After those few nightmare minutes, it was a face he would never forget. Perhaps that's why it seemed familiar.

"Not at the farm?" suggested the policeman. "Or in Flaxton somewhere? Football match, perhaps?"

Matt shook his head. He didn't watch football and he had seen nobody at the farm except the taciturn Cyril.

"Well, lets us know if it comes to you," said the policeman. He turned to Mrs Jessup. "How did this man get in, my dear?"

"He knocked on the front door," said Mrs Jessup. "I thought it was the children—Rachel wanted to interview me. I had the tape recorder all ready." Her eyes suddenly brimmed with tears and the cup rattled in its saucer as her hands shook. "He pushed me into the sitting room. I tried to stop him . . ." She couldn't say any more.

The policewoman leaned forward and retrieved the cup and saucer from Mrs Jessup. "It's all right," she said gently.

"He took my tape recorder," said Mrs Jessup, distraught. "And I wanted it for Rachel. All my old photos—why did he want those? He never knew those people."

"He didn't get away with it," the policewoman told her. "The children found the bag. Everything's safe."

"Even the teapot!" said Rachel, holding it up.

"Bang go the fingerprints," said the policeman ruefully, "but there'll be plenty on the other stuff." He nodded at Mrs Jessup's bruised face and added, "What about all this?"

"I have a few bits of jewellery," said Mrs Jessup with shaky dignity. "And I lock the drawer they're kept in. Silly, I suppose, but on tour you have to look after your bits and pieces. Gets to be a habit."

Matt was relieved to see that she had stopped shivering and seemed a bit more like her old self.

"Not silly at all," said the policeman. "I wish more people would keep their valuables safe."

"He went into my bedroom," said Mrs Jessup. "I heard him banging about—I went into the hall to try and ring the police but he heard the phone ting and he—he—" She indicated her grotesque face with a kind of embarrassment.

"Then he wanted the key, I suppose," put in the policewoman.

"Yes," said Mrs Jessup. "He guessed it was in my handbag. And it was. But he couldn't find it. So he tried to make me tell him where it was." She gave a little gasp which was half a laugh and half a sob. "It was only under the cushion." She leaned forward a little and groped beside her, producing a soft leather handbag. "Silly man," she said.

"You were lucky the children came when they did," said the policeman gravely.

"Oh, yes," said Mrs Jessup. "I was very lucky." But her bruised, swollen face with the blood drying on her chin made the words seem ironic.

"You'd be better in hospital for a day or two, my dear," said the policewoman firmly. "That cut may need stitching and you'll need someone to keep an eye on you for a bit. It'll take you some time to get over the shock."

"I don't like hospitals," said Mrs Jessup.

"But you don't want to be alone," said the policewoman. "Have you got any relatives who can come and look after you?"

"No need to bother people," said Mrs Jessup.

"What about your son?" suggested Rachel, with a glance at the policewoman to suggest that she might reinforce this idea. "He came to see you yesterday, didn't he? Where does he live?"

"Only in Flaxton," said Mrs Jessup, "but—"

"I'll give him a ring," said the policewoman, even more firmly. "He'll be very cross if he finds out this has happened and you didn't tell him. Now, what's his number?"

While Mrs Jessup was reluctantly dictating her son's address and telephone number, the red-haired policeman was looking round the room at the photographs. "Oh!" he said with interest, stopping at a signed picture of the dark-haired girl wearing a gauzy net skirt and a headdress of flowers. "Dodie Lamont! My dad's always on about her. She was his number one pin-up when he was a lad."

"Then he shall have my autograph," said Mrs Jessup with a queenly lift of her chin which made the battered face seem even more pitiful. "When my silly hands have stopped shaking."

The policeman laughed in amazement. "You mean *you're* Dodie Lamont! Good Lord! The old man will be thrilled to bits!"

"I still have my fans," said Mrs Jessup, smiling.

Rachel clasped her hands and gave a happy sigh. "Isn't that *lovely*," she said.

CHAPTER 9

A Well-Flung Bike

Much later that night, Matt yawned hugely. "I'll never get my maths homework done," he said. "I just can't think straight." The police had only just gone. He sipped his cocoa. It was very hot.

"When's your homework got to be in?" asked his mother.

"First thing tomorrow," said Matt. "Mr Watts." He groaned.

"Then I shall write Mr Watts a note," said his mother firmly. "And you're going straight to bed."

"He'll be furious," said Matt with some satisfaction. As he went on drinking his cocoa he thought about the evening's events. Mrs Jessup's son had arrived to take the old lady to stay with him and his wife for a while, then Matt had cycled home to explain to his startled mother that the police would be round shortly. It had been explained to him that people of Matt's age had to have any statement they made agreed by a parent. So there had been a lot more painstaking reading aloud and signing each page, and Matt presumed that the same thing was going on in Rachel's house. The policeman had checked by radio that the red Escort did in fact belong to Silcox and Waggitt, the agricultural suppliers, then wanted to know if Matt had ever been to their depot where he could have seen the man who made his escape in the car. Matt had shaken his head regretfully. Even now, he wasn't sure about the man's face. He saw it again in his mind's eye; a heavy face with black eyes under thick eyebrows, the mouth an almost lipless slit in the dark-stubbled skin. And the chin had a groove down the centre which looked like a deep pencil line, almost as if the man had two small chins pushed together to form one single one.

Thinking about the man's face, Matt relived the awful moment when he had looked through Mrs Jessup's kitchen window and seen what was going on. For a minute his stomach almost jibbed at the cocoa; but it was all right now. He was at home, in his own kitchen.

"Come on, finish that up," said his mother. "You're falling asleep where you sit."

There was tremendous excitement on the bus the next morning. Rachel's account of the events at Mrs Jessup's house left breakfast television absolutely nowhere, Matt thought.

"How *dreadful*!" said Sue, agog with interest and horror. "Poor old soul! But what did you *do*?"

"I thought at first the man was going to attack us," said Rachel dramatically. "He sort of crouched like a wild beast. But we stood our ground and he started to back away. We just fixed him with our eyes and didn't stop staring at him. Actually," she added, "I think he thought we'd got parents or something waiting for us outside."

Matt smiled inwardly at Rachel's account, remembering her hand clutching the back of his anorak as she peered nervously over his shoulder.

"So what did he *do*?" demanded Stephen.

"Turned and ran," said Rachel. "Straight out of the front door. He got in the car—here, but I haven't told you the best bit! He was driving the red Ford Escort! You know, the one I took the number of the other day when it was here in the car park. The one that Matt saw at Bill's farm."

"*And* the man had a bandage on his arm," put in Matt. "We didn't see it, but I did notice he held his hand up across his chest as if it hurt. Mrs Jessup saw the bandage under his coat."

Danny gave a slow whistle of amazement, and Stephen said, "So the bloke works at Silcox and Waggitt?"

"We don't know," said Matt. "The police said they'd be checking."

"Dead right they've been checking," said Stephen. "They were up at ours first thing this morning, wanting to talk to George. He was still in bed but they made Mum get him up."

There was a sudden, awful silence.

"What did they say?" asked Rachel, trying to sound casual.

"Asked him what he was doing at North's farm," said Stephen indignantly, "and where he was the night the school got done and the next day at the time someone tried to break into North's. Then they showed him a whole lot of pictures of various blokes, wanting to know if he knew any of them."

"And did he?" asked Danny.

"Well, yes, one or two," said Stephen guardedly. "Bound to, wasn't he? I mean, everyone round here goes to Mill Green, so some of those blokes were at school with George. No harm in that."

"Of course not," said Matt at once, trying to suppress the awful suspicion which had leapt into his mind. "I expect it's just a bit of police routine. Everyone knows it wouldn't be George."

"Don't know about everyone," said Stephen, not smiling. "But thanks, all the same."

Rachel and Matt exchanged a swift glance. There was no need to say anything. If Kritz and Plum were no longer serious suspects, the spy at Mill Green remained unknown. And George, whose disreputable friends still had younger brothers and sisters in the school, fitted the bill horribly well.

"But how could somebody else have got hold of the chemicals man's car?" Sue was saying.

"Might have stolen it," said Danny.

"Or he could have borrowed it," said Matt, who had been giving some thought to this problem. He was glad to abandon his unhappy speculations about Stephen's brother. "Suppose the man from Silcox and Waggitt—Mr Parsons—was involved in the previous thefts in some way? Even if he didn't do the actual stealing, he could have tipped someone else off. And if so, then the thieves are friends of his. And he'd lend his car to a friend, wouldn't he?"

Rachel frowned. "It doesn't tie up," she said. "Okay, it could have been him and his friends on the previous occasions, but how could he possibly have known about poor little Mrs Jessup and her silver photograph frames?" She went on quickly, "If there *is* an obvious suspect, it's me! I'd been going on about Mrs Jessup for days."

Matt knew that she too was trying to suppress her suspicions of George. "And me, don't forget," he put in. "*And* I'd been at North's the very day before it got done."

"Oh, don't be silly," said Sue. "You'd never do anything really *bad*, Matt. You'd blush at the very idea. Everyone knows you're an absolute goody-goody."

Matt blushed now, to his own annoyance and everyone else's amusement. To change the subject, he said, "I don't know what Mr Hazzard's going to say. He was pretty annoyed yesterday because we'd been to the police before telling him first."

"But it's nothing to do with him this time," Rachel argued. "Mrs Jessup isn't at his school and what we do out of school is our own affair."

"It seems to me nothing's your own affair," said Matt rather gloomily. "Whatever you do, somebody's interested."

"At least it lets Creepy and Plum out," said Sue. "What happened at Mrs Jessup's was nothing to do with them. I'm quite glad, really."

"I don't know so much," said Rachel thoughtfully. "Old Kritz did seem quite nice yesterday in a weird sort of way, but that doesn't mean he couldn't have been involved. Lots of people at school knew I was going to interview Mrs Jessup, didn't they? I tried to keep quiet about it but—well, I'm not a very quiet sort of person."

"Telling us!" said Danny. Rachel aimed a swipe at him and he ducked. "Let's face it," Rachel went on, "the staff talk to each other same as we do. I bet that staff room is a real old gossip-shop. And I'd told several of the teachers about Mrs Jessup having been a music hall artiste and all the lovely things she'd got."

"Which teachers?" asked Sue.

Rachel hesitated. "Only the nice ones," she admitted. "Mr Potter and Mrs Palgrave and people like that. I'm not saying it would be any of *them*," she added quickly, "just that they might have happened to mention it in the staff room and someone else might have overheard."

"Like Creepy or Plum," supplied Stephen. Matt looked at him. Was he trying to keep the old suspicions alive in order to protect his bother? Much as he liked Stephen, Matt could not rekindle any genuine suspicions of Kritz. It seemed that nobody else could, either, because there was a brooding silence which lasted while the bus slowed down and turned in at the gates of the school.

Matt was staring out of the window as the bus nosed its way along the drive toward the clutter of machinery and buckets and piles of sand where several men stood warming their hands round a small fire of scrap wood. The drive really did seem to be pretty well finished. Matt said, "It's looking quite—" and then stopped.

"Hey," said Danny, thumping his friend in the back, "what were you going to say?"

"That man," said Matt. "The one in the donkey jacket, over by the van. With his hand on the other man's arm. It's him. I know it is. So *that's* where I'd seen him!"

"Where?" demanded Rachel, jumping up from her seat across the gangway, "Matt, *where*?"

The bus was almost at a standstill. As if aware that he was being looked at, the man stopped arguing with the van's owner and turned round—and Matt found himself staring straight into the black eyes. The narrow mouth and deeply-cleft chin were like a remembered nightmare. "Stop the bus!" Matt shouted. "I've got to get off!"

He scrambled over Danny's legs, ignoring his small friend's shouts of protest about his grazed knees. Looking back over his shoulder he saw that the man had recognised him. He had taken to his heels, running back along the drive towards the gate.

"He's going to get away!" screamed Rachel. Matt was already at the front of the bus, shaking the driver by the arm. "Open the door!" he shouted frantically. "I've got to get out—*please*!"

Grumbling, the driver brought the bus to a halt and pulled the lever to open the door. Matt leapt out, followed by Rachel, and set off down the drive after the man, who was a long way ahead of them, running hard. Matt realised with despair that there was no hope of catching him.

A bicycle turned in through the gate. It was an old-fashioned, heavily built machine with a briefcase strapped to the carrier, ridden in an upright style by a figure in a tightly belted coat and a Tyrolean hat. It was Kritz.

"Stop that man!" yelled Matt, still running. "Mr Kritz! Stop him! He's the thief!" Even as he pounded along the drive, doubt sprang into Matt's mind. *Was* Kritz the spy? Did he know the man? If so, he would do nothing to stop him.

Kritz dismounted and trotted a few paces beside his bicycle, then came to a halt, staring in perplexity at the man tearing towards him.

"Stop that man!" Matt yelled again, and Rachel joined in from behind him, "Mr Kritz! Do stop him!"

Until the last moment, Matt thought Kritz was going to let the man go. Then, as the dark-jacketed figure approached at its lopsided run with a hand extended as to ward off any interference, Kritz hurled his bicycle into the man's path. It hurtled broadside into the man's legs and brought him crashing down onto the newly surfaced drive. The man tried to struggle up but he had one leg trapped under the crossbar and the bike slewed round him with its bell tinging in senseless warning as he tried to kick himself free.

Another figure ran in through the gate and grabbed at the bike as if to lift it clear of the man's legs. It was Terry Skinner.

"You leaving that alone!" Kritz shouted at him.

Terry turned and aimed a punch at Kritz but, to Matt's amazement, the lab technician was quicker. He grabbed Terry's outflung arm by the wrist and swung the boy round by it so that he sailed through the air and landed flat on his back. By this time Matt and Rachel had caught up with the scene, followed by most of their friends from the bus. Terry Skinner started to get painfully to his feet, but Matt heard the man shout, "Keep out of it, Terry—you'll only make things worse." Then he managed to scramble free of the bike and took a couple more lunging steps towards the gate.

Matt flung himself at the man but only succeeded in grabbing the back of his donkey jacket. The man turned to shake him off and Matt, seeing a car coming in rather fast through the gate, shouted, "Look out!"

The car skidded as the driver braked hard. Matt leapt aside, but the man crashed into the car's bonnet and was for a moment draped across it like a flag over a coffin. Then, as the car came to a halt, the man slid slowly to the ground and lay there, groaning. The driver jumped out, and Matt saw to his horror that it was Mr Watts.

Terry suddenly took to his heels, making for the space between the car and the gatepost, but Mr Watts collared him neatly. "Skinner, are you responsible for this?" he roared. "Who is this man?"

Terry pushed Mr Watts away violently. His face was ashen white as he stared at the man on the ground. "You flaming idiot," he said. "That's my father."

CHAPTER 10

The Odd Couple

Once again, Matt found himself in Mr Hazzard's office, this time with Rachel and P.C. Burkett, who was sitting on a chair with his cap in his hands. Somehow the policeman looked bigger and more solid than any of the teachers, Matt thought. Perhaps it was something to do with the uniform. Teachers wore vague, brownish clothes; by contrast, P.C. Burkett's hard-edged navy blue serge and shining silver buttons were quite startling.

The policeman smiled. "We meet again," he said. "What about the other little girl? Isn't she involved this time?"

"Sue? Not really," said Rachel. "It was just me and Matt that went to Mrs Jessup's."

"I was thinking more of this morning's incident," said P.C. Burkett, "concerning young master Skinner and his dad."

"Oh. Well—we were all there really," said Matt. "But the others were a bit longer getting off the bus."

The policeman nodded. "I see," he said. Then he smiled again and said, "But it was your quick action that collared the villian, I gather. I want to congratulate you on a good piece of work. We'd have got him all right—following an interview with Mr Parsons we'd just been round to Skinner's house and found out where he worked. But you were on the spot. Well done."

"Yes, indeed," agreed Mr. Hazzard. "And from my own point of view, I am delighted that all members of my staff are, of course, completely exonerated." He gave Matt and Rachel a straight look, and Matt blushed. Anxious to change the subject, he said, "Is Mr Skinner all right, sir? Not that I care a lot after what he did to Mrs Jessup, but—Mr Watts did sort of run him over."

"He wasn't badly hurt," said the policeman. "Just winded."

Rachel was bursting with curiosity. "I want to know all about it," she said. "The spy was Terry, was it? He'd know about the television camera and the VTR and he told his dad. But what about the farm—and what about Mrs Jessup? Oh!" She suddenly saw the answer to her own question and turned to Matt. "Aren't I an idiot! Friday breaktime, in the afternoon. We were sitting on that bench, weren't we, and he came and pulled my hair. I was telling you about Mrs Jessup then. He must have heard."

Matt nodded, remembering. "We went on talking because we were trying not to take any notice of Terry." He thought of Mrs Jessup's face and added, "I wish we hadn't."

"So do I," agreed Rachel. There was a pause. Then Rachel added, "But what about Bill's farm? Terry can't have known about Mr North's hi-fi stuff. Or did he?"

"Ah," said P.C. Burkett, "that's where your other suspect comes in. Mr Parsons. We picked him up this morning."

"I was sure it had something to do with him," said Matt. "But why did he lend his car to Terry Skinner's father?"

The policeman glanced at Mr Hazzard as if seeking the Headmaster's agreement that Matt and Rachel should hear this part of the story. Mr Hazzard considered for a moment, then made up his mind. "You may as well hear exactly what happened," he said, "because there are bound to be all sorts of rumours and garbled versions flying about, and it's better to know the truth of it. From what P.C. Burkett tells me, it's a sad story and an all-too-common one. Mr Parsons had a good job with Silcox and Waggitt but he had one fatal weakness. He was a gambler. That's to say, he couldn't resist betting money on horse races. When he lost, as gamblers inevitably do sooner or later, he was in deep financial trouble. Now, he and Mr Skinner were friends, I think on the basis of using the same pub. Mr Skinner always seemed to have plenty of money, for reasons which have now become painfully clear."

Matt and Rachel nodded. "Other people's money," said Rachel. "So he lent some to Mr Parsons?"

"A lot of money," Mr Hazzard agreed. "And this put him into quite a position of power over Mr Parsons. If someone asks you for a favour and you owe them a lot of money, you can hardly refuse, can you?"

"I see," said Matt thoughtfully. "So Mr Parsons had to become a sort of spy, passing on information about any house he went to that had valuable things in it."

"You've got it," said P.C. Burkett. "There have been several robberies at farms lately—you wouldn't have known, because it didn't concern the school in any way. Investigations are still going on, of course, but I'm pretty sure they're all connected."

"What about the car?" asked Rachel. "Why didn't Mr Skinner drive his own car? Why borrow the red Escort?"

"Mr Skinner," said the policeman ominously, "was banned from driving four months ago following a very nasty hit-and-run accident in which he was proved to be under the influence of alcohol."

"Drunken driving," said Rachel. "As well as everything else."

"So I suppose he thought he wouldn't be noticed so easily if he drove someone else's car," said Matt. "Because the registration number of his own would be known to the police."

"Exactly," agreed P.C. Burkett. "He only came back here this morning to try to borrow a van from one of his mates. I suppose he thought it was his only chance of making a getaway, but thanks to you it came to nothing. We've had reports of a red Escort being seen in suspicious circumstances once or twice before, but nobody's ever reported the number."

Rachel beamed proudly. Then she asked, "But what's going to happen? And what about our camera and things?"

"We're interviewing a certain gentleman in Birmingham about those," said P.C. Burkett. "I think he'll probably remember where they are. As to our villians—Skinner is remanded in custody until his case comes up, and Parsons is on bail."

"What'll happen to them?" asked Rachel.

"That's for the court to decide," said P.C. Burkett. "But I shall be surprised if we see much of Mr Skinner for quite some time."

Matt said, "I wish there was some way to make really *sure* he wouldn't do anything like that again." He remembered Mrs Jessup's battered face and felt the wave of queasiness rise again as he thought of it.

As if reading his thoughts, Rachel said, "I feel so awful about poor Mrs Jessup. If I hadn't talked about the interview I was going to do, Terry wouldn't have overheard and—it wouldn't have happened." She looked at Mr Hazzard and said, "You should have seen her face, sir."

"I know," said Mr Hazzard. "I've been in touch with her son to offer my apologies for any part the school may have inadvertently played in this dreadful business. As to the social survey—I think we'll forget it. When we get the VTR and camera back, we'll think of a different idea."

For a moment Rachel looked disappointed and Matt almost smiled. Despite what she had just said, Rachel had been very keen on the idea of interviewing Mrs Jessup.

But Rachel had already brightened up. She turned to Mr Hazzard and said, "I tell you what, sir! Let's do an old-fashioned music hall!"

Matt groaned.

Mr Potter slapped the register down on his desk and collapsed into his chair. "*I* don't know," he said. "Of all the forms in the school, why did I have to get saddled with you lot? Take my eye off you for half a minute and you're out there playing cops and robbers with real robbers."

"And real cops," said Rachel cheerfully. "Go on, sir, you know you love it."

"Don't be cheeky," said Mr Potter. "And, John, *will* you put those oranges down? I feel as if I'm in a demented marmalade factory."

"I got to get good at something," said John in an aggrieved tone.

"You're great at watching 'Superman'," said Michael.

John shrugged modestly. "Not the same, is it?" he said. "Not what you'd call a *skill*."

Marcia wiggled her newly varnished nails in the air to dry them. "You can see what he means," she remarked. "Same with me, innit? Think I'll do Beauty. Open a shop where you can get your hair dyed all different colours. Orange and pink and that. Blokes, too. And John can be a juggler with a circus."

"I'll go into farming with Dad," said Bill, carrying on the theme, "And Stephen will grub about on his small holding—"

"At least my eggs will be free-range!" said Stephen cheerfully. He could not stop smiling since the news about the spy had been announced.

"And I'll be an architect," said Danny. "I still reckon I could build a drive the right width in the first place. Rachel will go on the stage—"

"Felicity will run a knitting shop," said Debbie, "and I want to get married and have lots of children. So who needs school?"

"I do," said Matt. Everyone laughed and Peter Box said, "What for?"

Secretly, Matt thought he would rather like to be a policeman—and he'd need exams for that. But he was pretty sure everyone would laugh if he said so, so he just said, "Well, if it wasn't for going to school all week, you wouldn't look forward to the weekend, would you?"

"Thank you for that crumb of comfort," said Mr Potter gloomily. He opened the register and selected a red pen. "Actually," he added, "I'm frightfully proud of you. But you're not to get swollen heads. Now. Aiken . . . Box . . . Chalmers . . . Chuff . . ."

"Oh!" said Stephen instead of answering his name, "I just thought of something!"

"Well, it can wait a minute," said Mr Potter, with his finger still under Stephen's name. When he had finished calling out the list and had entered the total he closed the register and said, "Right. Let's have the latest brainwave."

"That bloke from Silcox and Waggitt," said Stephen. "I bet they'll sack him, won't they? I mean, he's a criminal."

Mr Potter hesitated. "From what I hear, it's more a

matter of being a bit misguided," he said. "Why do you ask?"

"Well, if they sack Mr Parsons, the next bloke down from him might step into his job," said Stephen. "And if he does, the bloke below him gets *his* job, and so on. So they'll need a new worker somewhere, won't they? Loading lorries or something."

"Quite probably," said Mr Potter.

"George could do it!" said Stephen. "He's ever so strong, and he can drive a forklift and a tractor and a bike and a car, and he knows about fertilisers and livestock and—"

"Stop, stop!" said Mr Potter. He smiled at Stephen. "Just for once," he said, "I may be able to do something useful. I don't know what Silcox and Waggitt intend to do about Mr Parsons, but it so happens that I know their personnel officer quite well. We were at college together. I see him from time to time and he did mention that they were expanding into prefabricated buildings, whatever those may be. Anyway, they'll be needing extra workers. I'll give him a ring this evening. Tell George to have a clean shirt ready and get his hair cut. He wants to look his best for the interview!"

"Oh, great!" said Stephen, beaming. "Thanks, sir—that's really terrific!"

"Think nothing of it," said Mr Potter modestly.

Mr Watts didn't say a word to Matt about his missing homework. Matt offered him the note his mother had written but Mr Watts waved it away irritably and said, "It's all right, boy." The lesson proceeded quietly, with none of the Senior Master's usual sarcasms.

Afterwards, Danny said, "Wasn't he down in the mouth! I bet he got a terrific telling-off from that policeman."

"What policeman?" asked Matt. This was somethng he knew nothing about.

"This morning," said Danny. "When you and Rachel had been told to go and see Mr Hazzard. There was a police van outside the gate but it couldn't get in because of old Watts's car. They'd got that bloke Skinner in handcuffs but he was shouting his head off about how Mr Watts had nearly killed him, and Terry was joining in. Well, they just shoved him in the van and they took Terry away in a police car but afterwards one of the policemen went up to Mr Watts and gave him a real talking-to about driving recklessly on school premises. He *does* come belting in if he's in a hurry. I wanted to listen but Mrs Abbott sent us in."

"Mr Watts's face was as red as anything, though!" chimed in Sue.

"Good," said Matt. "Now he knows what it feels like."

"What what feels like?" asked Danny.

"Being told off," said Matt. "By Mr Watts."

The rest of the day seemed unbearably flat and Matt was glad when the last bell went and he walked out to the bus park with the others. The late autumn sun hung like a red ball behind the thinning trees.

"We'll go and see Mrs Jessup again when she comes back from her son's," said Rachel. "Even if we're not doing the social survey."

"Oh, yes," agreed Matt. "Of course we will. I never fixed her shelf."

Rachel suddenly gave Matt a nudge and he turned to see what she meant. Kritz was walking past them, pushing his bicycle.

"Good night, sir!" Rachel called politely. Kritz paused in some surprise, then raised the green Tyrolean hat with a cockade of feathers in the side of it and replied, "Good night!"

Matt felt a pang of conscience. "Mr Kritz," he said, approaching, "is your bike all right? I mean, after this morning and everything?" He knew he was blushing, but he struggled on. "I thought it was terrific, the way you stopped the man."

"Thank you," said Kritz. He suddenly smiled. "This morning when you are shouting to me I am thinking, the boy is gone mad. And then I am looking at the man and thinking, no, it is the man who is mad." He shrugged and smiled again. "So I am throwing the bicycle."

"But is your bike okay?" asked Rachel.

Kritz patted the bicycle's saddle affectionately. "These old bicycles is very strong. No, she is all right. I walk always to the gate. It is safer so, with the children all about." And, with another courteous lift of his hat, he walked on down the drive.

"He's really rather a dear, in a way," said Rachel, gazing after him. "But I still can't think what he and Miss Plum had their heads together about when you saw them in the café, Matt."

"Neither can I," said Matt, watching the rather quaint figure making its way with the bicycle towards the gate. "It still seems a bit funny."

As Kritz reached the gate, someone who had been waiting outside stepped into view. "It's Miss Plumforth!" exclaimed Rachel.

The driver of the Tavenham bus leaned out of his window and shouted, "Come on, you kids! I've had enough mucking about!"

"Sorry!" Rachel shouted back. "Hang on!" They ran back to the bus and climbed on board and the driver shut the doors and started the engine.

As the bus moved slowly down the drive Rachel was staring intently through the window, and Matt, too, felt a prickle of curiosity about the odd couple. Miss Plumforth wasn't at Mill Green on Tuesdays. So why was she hanging round the gate today, a Tuesday? Surely they couldn't have been wrong about her and Kritz, after all? It didn't seem possible. And, Matt discovered, he didn't *want* it to be possible.

"Oh!" said Rachel as the bus pulled out of the gate and started down the Tavenham road. "Matt, look!"

The two people who walked along the grass verge in the fading daylight, pushing the old-fashioned bicycle, were holding hands.

Matt laughed and blushed and laughed again. "I'm such a twit!" he said. "I never thought of that!"

Everyone else stood up and stared out as well and, amid the whistles and jocular remarks, Matt could hear in his imagination what Rachel was going to say. He was right. "I think it's *lovely*," she said.

Matt groaned and Rachel smiled unrepentantly. "Go on, Matt," she said. "It is, isn't it? I bet you think so, too!"

Matt glanced once more out of the window, but the bus had rounded a bend and the couple were out of sight.

He gave a little sigh as he turned back to the brightly lit interior of the bus. "It'll be just an ordinary day tomorrow," he said. "I'd better do that homework for Mr Watts."

MILL GREEN

School Series

by Alison Prince

Now there's a great new school series in Armada.

Mill Green is a big, new comprehensive – with more than its fair share of dramas and disasters! Get to know Matt, Danny, Rachel, and the rest of the First Form mob in their first two exciting adventures.

Mill Green on Fire

When someone starts fires in the school and blames the caretaker, Matt is determined to catch the real culprit. But his brilliant plan to catch the firebug goes horribly wrong . . .

Mill Green on Stage

The First Formers prepare for the Christmas pantomime – and sparks soon fly when Marcia Mudd, a ghastly new girl, gets the best part. But when Matt locks Marcia in a cupboard and she disappears from the school, there's big trouble for everyone . . .

A Spy at Mill Green

The school is stunned when its brand-new video recorder and television camera are stolen. With all the clues pointing to an inside job, the First Formers turn detective . . .

More stories about Mill Green will be published in Armada.

Kay Tracey Mysteries

by Frances K. Judd

Look out for Armada's fantastic new detective series!

Kay Tracey has an uncanny talent for solving clues and unravelling baffling mysteries. Don't miss her first two thrilling adventures.

1 The Double Disguise
2 In the Sunken Garden

Armada

'JINNY' BOOKS

by Patricia Leitch

FOR LOVE OF A HORSE

When Jinny Manders rescues Shantih, a chestnut Arab, from a cruel circus, her dream of owning a horse seems to come true. But Shantih escapes on to the moors.

A DEVIL TO RIDE

Shantih, safe at last, is inseparable from Jinny. But the Arab is impossible to ride.

THE SUMMER RIDERS

Jinny is furious when Marlene, a city girl, comes to stay. But when Marlene's brother gets into trouble with the police, only Jinny and Shantih can help him.

NIGHT OF THE RED HORSE

When archaeologists excavate an ancient site, Jinny and Shantih fall under the terrifying power of the Celtic 'Pony Folk'.

GALLOP TO THE HILLS

When Ken Dawson's dog, Kelly, is wrongly accused of killing sheep, Jinny is determined to save him. But will she be in time?

HORSE IN A MILLION

Jinny is heart-broken when Shantih disappears one night. Desperate to find her, Jinny begins a dangerous search.

THE MAGIC PONY

Jinny's life is full of problems when she rescues an aged white pony. But an ancient magic intervenes.

RIDE LIKE THE WIND

Finmory House is to be sold, and Jinny and Shantih must go back to the city. How can Jinny save the home she loves?

Armada

THE EVEN MORE AWFUL JOKE BOOK

Compiled by Mary Danby

It's worse than ever!

Drive your family and friends up the wall with this fantastic new collection of glorious groaners, rib-tickling riddles, horrendous howlers and crazy cartoons. Here are a few sickly samples to whet your appetite . . .

Did you hear about the lady who wired up her electric blanket to a toaster?
She kept popping out of bed all night.

JIMMY: I'm sorry I'm late, sir, but I was having a dream about a football match.
TEACHER: Why did that make you late?
JIMMY: They played extra time.

Why did the wagon train stop in the middle of the prairie?
It had Injun trouble.